W9-BCG-595

Be a New Christian all your life!

In these pages, Ray Ortlund addresses the most common problems Christians face: doubts about salvation, the "same old sins," getting bogged down and discouraged...

Be a New Christian All Your Life is for both the new in faith and mature believers — all Christians who want to stay fresh with God.

In chapters filled with candid anecdotes and humorous cartoons, the author constantly shows, "It's a great thing to be open and humble and continually fresh in your relationship with God Almighty."

To read *Be a New Christian All Your Life* is to want to grow, to want a stronger faith, to be positively assured of good things to come.

Be A NEW CHRISTIAN All Your Life

Be A
NEW
CHRISTIAN
All Your
Life

RAYMOND C. ORTLUND

Power Books

Fleming H. Revell Company
Old Tappan, New Jersey

Permission to quote from "Cookies" in *Frog and Toad Together* by Arnold Lobel is gratefully acknowledged. Copyright © 1971, 1972 by Arnold Lobel. Reprinted by permission of Harper & Row, Publishers, Inc.

Unless otherwise identified, Bible quotations in this book are taken from the Holy Bible, New International Version. Copyright © 1973, 1978, 1984 International Bible Society. Used by permission of Zondervan Bible Publishers.

Library of Congress Cataloging-in-Publication Data

Ortlund, Raymond C.
    Be a new Christian all your life / Raymond C. Ortlund.
        p.   cm.
    Rev. ed. of: Be a new Christian all your life. 1983.
    Includes bibliographical references.
    ISBN 0-8007-5368-2
    1. Christian life—Presbyterian authors. I. Title. II. Title:
Be a New Christian all your life.
BV4501.2.O733   1990
248.4'851—dc20   90-37035
                                                           CIP

All rights reserved. No part of this publication may be reproduced, stored in a retrieval system, or transmitted in any form or by any means—electronic, mechanical, photocopy, recording, or any other—except for brief quotations in printed reviews, without the prior permission of the publisher.

Copyright © 1983, 1990 by Raymond C. Ortlund
Published by the Fleming H. Revell Company
Old Tappan, New Jersey 07675
Printed in the United States of America

To my sons
Ray, Jr., and Nels
and to my sons-in-law
Walt Harrah and John McClure III
Fine young men who are helping me
stay renewed

Contents

Be A NEW CHRISTIAN All Your Life

ONE

Lord, Keep Before Me a Vision of Where I'm Going

For background, first read Habakkuk 1:1—2:4; 3:16-19

HERMAN

"The man we're looking for will be dynamic and aggressive."

Copyright, 1976, Universal Press Syndicate. Reprinted with permission. All rights reserved.

> Life is like a
> parachute jump.
>
> You've got to get it
> right the first time.

Andrew Carnegie was once asked the secret of his enormous success. He said, "I owe it all to my flashes."

His friends said, "What do you mean by flashes?"

Carnegie said, "Well, all my life I've waked up early in the morning, and there comes to my mind a waking flash, telling me what to do that day. If I follow those waking flashes, I always succeed."

I want you to get a vision, as you read this book, which isn't a hunch or a flash—some kind of innate ability to do the right thing in business—but which is for you a new, Spirit-given insight into God's wonderful and specific plan for your life·

God Wants to Give You a Vision

He has a plan for you, and He wants to show it to you with specific enough shape that you can follow it.

He has always told His children what He wants them to do.

He told Adam to have children and to tend a garden.

He told Noah to build an ark to preserve a godly line of descendants.

He told Abraham to move to a new land and establish his family there.

He told Moses to lead the children of Israel out of Egypt

He told Joshua to lead them into Canaan.

He told Solomon to build Him a temple.

He told Isaiah and Jeremiah and Paul to preach.

What has He told you to do?

Have you recently had a fresh word from the Lord to renew

your sense of direction and purpose, to motivate you, steady you, comfort you, and fill you with courage and hope and plans? Ephesians 5:10 says to "find out what pleases the Lord." He gives each believer ways to please Him that are different from anyone else's. He had reasons for making you that He didn't have for anyone else, and He tells you to find out what they are.

Four Proofs That God Has Special Purposes for You

1. Long ago God made you—specifically you, my friend. Says David to God in Psalm 139:13 and 16:

> For you created my inmost being;
>   you knit me together in my mother's womb . . .
>   your eyes saw my unformed body.
> All the days ordained for me
>   were written in your book
>   before one of them came to be.

2. Long ago God determined your very own life span:

> Men's days are determined;
>   you have decreed the number of his months,
>   and have set limits he cannot exceed (Job 14:5).

3. Long ago God planned the path for your individual life. Hebrews 12:1 says to "run with perseverance the race marked out for [you]"—a piece of track no one else can run over, not even your identical twin. Only you will ever live your life.

4. And long ago God decided what good things only you would do:

> [You] are God's workmanship, created in Christ Jesus to do good works, which God prepared in advance for [you] to do (Ephesians 2:10).

How to Find God's Vision for Your Life

If you are that uniquely special to God—

Be very careful, then, how you live—not as unwise but as wise, making the most of every opportunity, because the days are evil. Therefore do not be foolish, but understand what the Lord's will is (Ephesians 5:15–17).

How can you understand what the Lord's will is—for you? Here's what Andrew Murray suggested:

Begin by asking God very humbly to give you, by the Spirit who dwells in you, the vision of . . . wholehearted love and obedience as it has been actually prepared for you in Christ. . . .
Ask earnestly, definitely, believingly, that God reveal this to you. Rest not until you know fully what your Father means you to be. . . .
When you begin to see [it]. . . offer yourself unreservedly to God.[1]

Wait on Him, my friend. Let Him speak to you through His Word. Give Him time.

I was a thirty-six-year-old pastor, weary and depleted, sitting alone on a big rock in Colorado—I know the very spot—and I prayed, "Lord, I need a new word from You."

And there before me in my Bible was Acts 1:8. Now, I know that verse was for the early disciples, but that day it was just for me:

You will receive power when the Holy Spirit comes on you; and you will be my [witness] . . . to the ends of the earth.

At that point I'd hardly been anywhere! The vision seemed so large in scope that for several months I was too embarrassed even to tell Anne. When I did, she got a big map for me with "Acts 1:8" printed on it, and red stickers ready.

Since that day God has let me minister, by radio or in person, on every continent of the world, over and over. I know I'm not much—but for three decades since, I've been thrilled and motivated by the vision for my life that God gave me that day in Colorado. And I have the feeling He's not at all through fulfilling it!

A young man once said to me, "You know, I don't care whether or not I get to be famous, but I do want to be significant." Don't you feel that way, too? And a great God has planned for your life to be highly significant—maybe not highly visible, but in the light of eternity, highly significant. Don't miss it!

Life is so short.

You only get one whack at it, my friend, one pass-through. There are no reruns, no instant replays. And soon you'll report in—maybe sooner than you think—and so will we all.

And then we'll all sit down to a banquet of consequences!

Three Commitments to Help Give Your Vision Shape

However God arranges your Christian life and moves you forward, it should be around three priorities.[2] These priorities will keep your dreams and goals from turning inward and becoming self-centered and self-feeding:

1. *Always make God Priority One.*

He must be first, first, first—with nothing and nobody as any near rival.

There were milling throngs in Jesus' day who called themselves "disciples" and occasionally sought his touch (Luke 6:19).

But there were twelve (and particularly three) who zealously stayed at His heart and side always, their eyes on Him to absorb

Him totally. Said Peter, "Lord, we have left everything to follow you" (Mark 10:28).

Christian, in this moment, if you haven't before, move from the milling throng to His inner circle. Stop your reading for a moment of prayer, and tell Him so.

There are future rewards for the twelve apostles in status, power, and glory which will absolutely dumbfound us all—but listen: making Him Priority One is reward enough!

Ask Him to forgive and cleanse you afresh and take you close to His heart—to live in His presence, to be your very self a continual offering of worship and praise.

Recently I drew up some new goals I particularly want to work on between now and next January 1. Fourteen of our family members are joining me! One of them is, "Vow that while you live, you will seek to live with enthusiasm and joy by the Holy Spirit." I'm making that a goal by taking a reading on myself every night to see if that day I sought to live like that! Well, on a scale of one to ten, I'm doing right now maybe between six and seven. If you ever meet me, reader, check on me and ask how I'm doing.

And I myself have a vision—for the readers of this book. I have a vision that in your daily schedule you will see Jesus Christ as Lord:

- that you will give Him the best of every day.
- that He will get the first "dibs" on your date book.
- that you will give Him absolute lordship over every conversation. (I like to say, "Lord, be Lord over every phone call that I do not know is coming, and every person I do not know I'll meet, as well as those I see who have appointments.")
- that He really will get the first crack at your checkbook.
- that there will not be one area of your life where He isn't Lord.

Enjoy His presence, love Him, thank Him, talk to Him, rejoice in Him, check in with Him, get orders from Him, praise Him all day long! You can go second class if you want to—but Jesus wants to bring you first class with greatest satisfaction!

I have a vision that the readers of these words will bow to the lordship of Jesus Christ, to make Him literally "Head over all things to the church"!

2. Make your fellow believers always Priority Two.

I have a vision that the readers of this book, many of you brand-new Christians, will truly learn to be the people of God in loving relationships.

Oh, if I could tell you how members of the body of Christ have loved me and helped me!

Several years ago I took a twelve-month sabbatical. God moved some of His people from here and there to remember that Anne and I would be without the close relationships of a pastorate. Not knowing one another, they reached out singly or by twos to ask if they could be in a small group with us. There were ten in all—really too many!—three other couples and two single women and Anne and me.

One evening a week they traveled unbelievable numbers of miles to worship the Lord together and support one another. One of the fellows was in a traveling job, and he'd fly into the Los Angeles airport and come directly to join us without dinner. Or he'd leave at the end of our time together and go catch a midnight flight for somewhere. One of the fellows was a counselor who, on that particular day of the week, always got up at 5:30 A.M. to drive 125 miles to work at a psychiatric hospital.

Nothing was ever said about being committed to one another. It simply wrapped us around. It bound us together with cords of love that the Holy Spirit Himself held strong. And at the end of that year, sort of like the days after Pentecost, God exploded us apart into separate ministries.

I have a vision that in your joys and needs, you'll be that cared for, that prayed for. Of course you'll love your church as a whole. Of course you'll be together on Sundays for worship and instruction and those larger relationships. But I also see you accountable to a special few others in a supportive fellowship. (For more study on these special groups, *see* my wife Anne's book *Discipling One Another.*[3])

Some Christians say, "My private life is no one else's business." Oh, yes, it is! It must be others' business—to pray for you and love you and support you.

Cain asked the question first: "Am I my brother's keeper?" Yes, yes, Cain! You were! You should have encouraged and helped and loved your brother Abel. You were responsible for his well-being and his success. You failed him!

3. *And make this needy world around you Priority Three.*

I have a vision that you readers of this book will so love God, and be so supported by your fellow Christians, that you'll reach out in courage, in suffering, and in patient, consistent love to the godless world around you.

They won't understand why you care. Your neighbors won't thank you; they'll probably just think you're some kind of religious nut or "Jesus freak." And the world overseas won't even know you at all. They'll never take a trip to come acknowledge your prayers and sacrifices on their behalf.

Then why get excited over the world's hurting ones?

What the Results Can Be When One Believer Has a Vision for the World

Let's look at the Old Testament prophet Habakkuk to see why. Habakkuk lived in a tougher day—in many ways—than we live in. He was a preacher in Judah during the reign of Manasseh, an absolutely vile and loathsome king. Manasseh built altars to pagan idols all over his country—even right inside God's very temple. He "practiced sorcery, divination and witchcraft, and consulted mediums and spiritists" (2 Chronicles 33:6), and to offer fire sacrifices he actually burned his own sons to death! Ugh!

We think we have trouble today, but King Manasseh was such

a huge influence that before long he'd carried all the people of Jerusalem and Judah with him into widespread, open, idolatrous practices and moral wickedness.

Second Chronicles 33:10, in the midst of all this garbage, is a pathetic verse: "The Lord spoke to Manasseh and his people, but they paid no attention."

How did He speak? Why, through His preacher Habakkuk. I've been a preacher long enough to tell you that preaching is hard enough when it's received—but when it's belittled it costs you everything you've got in spiritual, emotional, and even physical resources.

So here's Habakkuk, feeling that as a believer he's ineffective, as a witness he's useless. And he cries to God:

How long, O Lord, must I call for help,
  but you do not listen?
Or cry out to you, "Violence!"
  but you do not save? . . .
Why do you tolerate wrong?
Destruction and violence are before me . . .
  conflict abounds . . .
the law is paralyzed,
  and justice never prevails (Habakkuk 1:2–4).

But when God's time is right—wham! The Assyrians sweep over Judah, killing and conquering, and put a hook in King Manasseh's nose and lead him as a captive off to Babylon.

So here's Manasseh in a Babylonian prison. Boy, is his nose sore! If he touches his finger to it, his eyes sting with tears.

"God," he says, "I totally goofed. How can I tell You how sorry I am?"

What, what, what? Can we believe our ears?

Yes, *King Manesseh repents.* I'll bet all Habakkuk's sermons are flooding back into his memory.

"God," prays the king, "Habakkuk said, 'Woe to him who builds his realm by unjust gain' [Habakkuk 2:9]. That's just what I did, Lord.

"He said, 'Woe to him who builds a city with bloodshed' [Habakkuk 2:12]. That was *my* sin! I see it clearly now. O God, I can't forget his words! I can't forget his life! He was right, I was wrong! O God, is it too late for me? Is it too late?"

"No," says the Lord of infinite tenderness and mercy, "it isn't too late for you, Manasseh."

Manasseh is returned to his kingdom (2 Chronicles 33:13).

He rebuilds Jerusalem's wall.

He fortifies the cities of Judah.

He gets rid of all the foreign gods!

He removes the idol in the temple of the Lord, as well as the altars! He throws them out of the city!

He restores the altar of the Lord and sacrifices fellowship offerings and thank offerings on it!

And he tells his people to do the same. A powerful king becomes humble and changes history.

Does the life of one believer—like Habakkuk—in a wicked society pay off? Well, what do you think?

The Fruits of Vision

When your witness for Christ is steady and clear, there are potent forces at work you can't dream of. There are the hidden maneuverings, the invisible but powerful strategies of the Spirit of God, constantly working because of your life.

Believer, get stars in your eyes! Understand that He can use you!

Get free of memories of past failures. Satan, the accuser of the brothers, will tell you that your future will be more of the same old baloney as the past. Don't believe him. Live to win (1 Corinthians 9:24).

Ask God for big things, as He reveals His visions to you

(1 Chronicles 4:9,10). "Make no little plans; they have no magic to stir men's blood."

Refuse to let anything hinder the fulfillment of your visions. Discipline yourself. Exercise self-control. You have everything you need in Jesus Christ for success. Center your ambitions on Him. Don't live on emotions. Let your self-will be broken. Bring your bodily appetites under control.

"Consecrate yourself, for tomorrow the Lord will do amazing things for you" (Joshua 3:5 paraphrase).

"Lord, if you have to break down any prisons of mine before I can see the stars and catch the vision, then, Lord, begin the process now.

"In joyous anticipation, AMEN."

—Catherine Marshall

*   *   *   *

May he give you the desire of your heart
   and make all your plans succeed.
We will shout for joy when you are victorious
   and will lift up our banners in the name of our God.
May the Lord grant all your requests (Psalm 20:4,5).

Questions for Review

1. What three commitments should help shape your vision of what God wants for your life? How can you make each of these practical, for you?

2. How are you different today from the way you were five years ago? How are you the same today as you were five years ago?
3. What in your life do you want to remain the same five years from now? What do you want to see changed in the next five years?

When our neighbor Betty was a brand-new Christian she and Anne made a pact never to become old Christians.

Never to get bored and pooh out.

Never to get hardened.

Never to get knowledgeable of other Christians' weaknesses.

Never to quit going hard after God.

Never to lose their love for His Word and for prayer.

For several years now they've prayed that for each other and occasionally checked each other on it; of course they don't get straight A's, but that's their desire and goal—to stay continually new with God.

"So then, just as you received Christ Jesus as Lord, continue to live in him" (Colossians 2:6).

TWO

Lord, I Want to Worship You From Now Till Forever

For background, first read Revelation 5:6–14

Your First Business: Worship

Some time ago *Fortune* magazine ran an article on that forty-seven-billion-dollar company, American Telephone and Telegraph. It seems that A T & T's chief executives were grumbling about themselves, "As the years go by your head becomes more and more bell-shaped."

So they asked themselves a basic question: "What is our business?" The leaders of one of the largest and richest companies in the world felt they had gotten away from their basic business.

It can happen to anybody. Christians can not only get away

from their basic business, which is to worship God, but plenty of them never learned it was their basic business in the first place! And thousands of churches have no idea that their primary function is supposed to be to worship God.

Let's go to Revelation 5 and get perspective on this.

We're not talking first of all about churchgoing, although that's part of it. We're talking about worship—your attitude as well as your action.

Christian, I want you to know how to love God! You see, God has made you as a person with energy, with intelligence, with skills, and with feelings and emotions. And if you don't spend these in your highest and strongest sense on God, you'll spend them on yourself. So you must learn to worship God or you'll become tragically man-centered.

> "To worship is:
>   To quicken the conscience by the holiness of God,
>   To feed the mind with the truth of God,
>   To purge the imagination by the beauty of God,
>   To open the heart to the love of God,
>   To devote the will to the purpose of God."
>   —Archbishop William Temple

Anne and I and a few others were on the island of Patmos in the Aegean Sea off Greece. (Patmos is the island the Apostle John was exiled to, and where he wrote the last book of the Bible, Revelation.)

Some of us climbed to the top of Patmos where there's a tiny monastery. Then we looked around in a cave where tradition says John wrote Revelation.

As our little tender was putt-putting us out over the blue water to our ship again I turned and looked at the rocky Patmos. And I thought, *Imagine John being shipped in, thrown ashore with a few belongings, and left as a prisoner on that island—maybe with a few other prisoners, probably criminals!* I thought, *Holy cow, what an awesome experience, being dumped on that big rock to live and die!*

But it was there that the pure and glorious Christ appeared to him. And he wrote a book to describe what happened: "The Revelation of Jesus Christ"! And it's crammed full of worship and praise!

Christian, *no matter what bad experience ever comes to you, the Christ of glory is always there, and it's always time to worship Him.*

Recently I went through deep waters—one of those tough experiences most pastors identify with sooner or later in ministry. With my letter of resignation in my hand I was driving down a road and this warming thought came to me: *Lord, if I never preach another sermon in my life, I want to worship You as long as I live, and I'll be totally fulfilled. I want to keep praising You.* I can't tell you how comforting the Lord was to me at that moment.

The Object of Your Worship

Wait! You're about to let your eye slip down the page. Don't! (You think I'm psychic? I could tell.) Why was your eye going to skip a little? Because I've been talking about you and me (more interesting), and I'm about to switch to Him (less interesting to us self-centered people). But you wouldn't admit that, even to yourself.

"Yes, yes," you're saying. "I know Ray Ortlund must of course put in a section on 'The Object of Our Worship' to round out the chapter, and—my goodness, yes, it's the most important part—but hmmm, I wonder what he's going to cover after these next few pages. . . . " Actually (maybe unconsciously) you're looking for the next part that deals with you again.

You've just hit on why true worship is so hard!

Watchman Nee says "to kneel before Him for an hour demands all the strength we possess. We have to be violent to hold that ground."

Listen, this could be the most crucial part of the book to you—just as worship should be the most crucial aspect of your life.

Right now, call on the Holy Spirit to make you hungry for Christ Himself.

All around you is the highly contagious and potentially fatal disease of self-occupation. Many are sick with it; maybe you've caught it too.

> Cry out for His strength to help you move
> outside yourself and seek Him!

Plead with Him to reveal Himself to you; search for the details of the perfection and strength and beauty of Christ in all their vividness! Beg Him, "Come, Lord Jesus"—not only for His bodily return to earth, but for His immediate coming into your admiring attention.

(When you see Him "high and lifted up," when you magnify Him as you learn of Him and draw close to Him, you yourself will be lifted and changed—but that's another subject. "And we, who with unveiled faces all reflect the Lord's glory, are being transformed into his likeness with ever-increasing glory, which comes from the Lord, who is the Spirit"—2 Corinthians 3:18.)

"Worthy" they call Him in Revelation 5.

"The Lion of the tribe of Judah." The Lion: "mighty among beasts, who retreats before nothing" (Proverbs 30:30). This is the only time Christ is ever called "the Lion," although two thousand years before, His ancestor Judah had been called "a lion's cub" (Genesis 49:9).

"The Root of David." *Root?* Humanly speaking, Christ was David's descendant, following David by a thousand years. How could He be his "Root"? As a matter of fact, Isaiah had prophesied that "a shoot will come up from the stump of Jesse [David's father]: from his roots a Branch will bear fruit" (Isaiah 11:1)—capital B on "Branch." But the magnificent, eternal Christ was also before David. He'd even created him (Colossians 1:16)! So Revelation ends with Jesus correctly saying about Himself, "I am the Root and the Offspring of David" (Revelation 22:16).

Dig. Dig deep. Look at Him. Discover some of the wonders of who He really is.

"He has triumphed!" says Revelation 5:5. "He is able to open the scroll and its seven seals." (Possible translation: He is the only One with the authority to unveil the plans of God.)

He is the Lamb!—the Sacrifice no longer limp in death but alive again and vital, standing glorious in the throne room.

He has seven horns and seven eyes! In other words He is perfect in strength and perfect in perception—all-powerful and all-seeing.

Such a One! Revelation seems like a far-out book, because it stretches us to realize that all He is and does is past describing in ordinary terms. He is "wow" and "sensational" beyond your wildest imaginings, and the way Christ is described you just want to gulp and shut your mouth and cringe in worship, at the very least. John, at the sight of Him, passed out altogether (Revelation 1:17).

Not knowing Him, not understanding who He is, people can be scandalously cocky and insulting before Him. R. A. Torrey, a Britisher who once pastored the Church of the Open Door in Los Angeles, was approached by a fellow who said, "Dr. Torrey, I'm not a Christian but I'm moral and upright. I'd like to know what you have against me?"

Mr. Torrey looked him in the eye and said, "I charge you, sir, with treason against the King of heaven!"

Jesus Christ is Lord over all. All must answer to Him. The gospel is His, and we must believe it and surrender to Him. All who live and breathe must ultimately fall on their knees and acknowledge who He really is, says Philippians 2:10,11—either in humble acceptance of Him now while there's time, or with bitter tears because they found out too late.

Bow at conversion, and keep bowing! Worship and keep worshiping! If you ever lose your sense of worship you'll lose reverence, joy, everything. You'll come to church as though you're coming to your Pal, Mr. Nice Guy. You'll ostensibly slap His back and say, "Well, here I am, you lucky Christ. I'm here to be a Good Boy, to pat myself on the back by going to church again and giving You a nod." But it won't work. Church will be a drag, and your life will be uncleansed, unrenewed.

No, no! Stay a new Christian all your life by never getting over the awe and wonder of Him. See the enormous cost of your salvation—that He was the Lamb slain; but see the great victory—that He is today the Lamb standing with seven horns and seven eyes, full of authority and wisdom and perception. Then you'll begin to sing "Amazing love! How can it be that Thou, my God, shouldst die for me?"

Your Attitude in Worship

Sunday morning is a reflection of all the rest of your week.

Christians who live self-centered lives all week—prayerless, hectic, self-dependent, exhausting—stagger into church without the foggiest idea of what they're supposed to do there. They may be dressed up and temporarily composed, but they don't know for what reason.

They don't understand their function, worship, and all they can do is try to "get something out of it." So they come saying, "Okay, Rev, you've got an hour and ten minutes. Fill 'er up!" But you see—

Church isn't a gas station. Jesus Christ isn't there to "service them."

Church isn't a routine between boxing rounds, for a little rubdown or water.

It isn't a pit stop.

Church is the strong place where we Christians are to gather and lift high our Lord and Savior. We seek to exalt Him all week long, but then once a week together we make a unified hallelujah to the Lamb of God who takes away our sins and is today alive and glorious.[4]

Revelation 5:8,9—"The four living creatures and the twenty-four elders fell down before the Lamb. Each one had a harp and they were holding golden bowls full of incense, which are the prayers of the saints. And they sang a new song. . . ."

When you come to worship, seek to meet God's needs first. In meeting His needs you will meet your own. God will see to that. (You can't put together a worship service by first studying people's needs; you have to study God's needs first.) "What are Your feelings, Lord? What do You desire?" And in studying God and what you think pleases Him, then you'll understand how to help yourself and others. Know what it is to bow before God, to "sing a new song" (maybe an old song, but fresh and new to you at that moment), to offer your praises right to Him, to minister to Him! Never mind what others are doing all around you; you can worship the Lord.

What is the attitude of worship? Well, it's an attitude of "coming near," of desire, of pressing in toward God, of longing for Him.

You must believe that it's possible for you to do this. Maybe you feel, "I don't have any right to come before a holy God. I feel so dirty, so unqualified. How can I come before Him?"

You have every right through Jesus Christ. We're all in the same condition: sinners saved by the grace of Christ. So you must believe that it's possible. Some people don't think God likes them; that's poor thinking about God. He welcomes you in the Lord Jesus! He loves you, and He wants you near to Him! Attitude is so important. To minister to God He must be very attractive to you.

David wanted to. In Psalm 27:4 he wrote, "One thing I ask of the Lord, this is what I seek: that I may dwell in the house of the

Lord all the days of my life, to gaze upon the beauty of the Lord and to seek him in his temple."

Give Him all your attention! God told the sons of Zadok who were priests to "stand before him" (Ezekiel 44:15), as if to be in readiness to attend to whatever He wants and needs; to stand before Him as a servant stands before his master, saying, "What can I do for You, God? Could I sing a hymn to You? How could I please You?"

We're normally such "antsy" people. Our slogan is "Don't just stand there, do something." But God is saying, "Don't just do something, stand there." Learn to be in the presence of God, to watch His face, to be attentive, ready to minister to Him.

Come early to church and get right to Him; friends can wait until afterward. Internalize all that happens: the organ music, the choir, the prayers, the preaching. . . Let it all be God's input to you alone, and your submissive, loving response to Him.

That's worship!

"We're to be worshipers first and workers only second. We take a convert and immediately make a worker out of him. God never meant it to be so. God meant that a convert should learn to be a worshiper, and after that he can learn to be a worker."

—A. W. Tozer

Worship Him at church weekly with His people. Worship Him all the rest of the week by your thoughts, your words, your deeds, your life. Lift your eyes from the humdrum; continually get to God, get to God!

There are three songs in Revelation 5, and then throughout the rest of the book as the drama unfolds there's one after another after another. They're outbursts of song and praise to the

Lamb! No wonder the book is so magnificent, and that's what will make your life magnificent!

Worship and praise! "Songs in the night" when you're down. Morning songs when you're up.

"Be filled with the Spirit," says Paul in Ephesians 5:18,19; "sing and make music in your heart to the Lord." Said the poet Carlyle, "Let me make a nation's song, and I care not who makes their laws."

Let successive outbursts of worship and song to God shape your entire Christian life!

They'll sustain your "first love."

They'll keep you new.

> Why don't you put this wonderful Revelation 5:6–14 in front of you and pray a prayer of worship to the Lord, letting your eye go down the page for inspiration to give you the words to say to Him?
> He'll enjoy that. So will you.

Questions for Review

1. How can the passages in Revelation which depict the Lord in glory aid us in our worship?
2. What does posture have to do with worship? What does attitude have to do with worship?
3. What can we do to enrich our participation in the church worship services?

THREE

Lord, Keep My Prayer Life Fresh

For background, first read Matthew 6:5–15

Yogi Berra, the great baseball catcher, was in crouched position, the game was tied and the moment was tense. Up came an opposing player to bat—a Roman Catholic like Yogi—and he took his bat and made a cross on the plate.

Yogi reached over and wiped the cross away and said, "Why don't we let God just watch this game?"

Maybe that's all right for baseball, but God wants to be totally involved in your life as a Christian, from moment to moment to moment. You mustn't ever move Him off to be a spectator. Not ever.

What will make you different from the world? The world puts

God in the bleachers and money and power in the field. So does a worldly Christian. But the only glory you'll ever know is the glory that comes from putting God in the center of where the action is, and everything else on the sidelines. He may give you money or power, but your heart will not be enamored with them.

This attitude isn't frightening or dangerous. It's the safest, wisest thing you can do.

> Paul: "I consider everything a loss compared to the surpassing greatness of knowing Christ Jesus my Lord, for whose sake I have lost all things. I consider them rubbish, that I may gain Christ and be found in him" (Philippians 3:8,9).

Everything but Christ must fade off to the periphery! He must become total focus!

In that life attitude you discover you're praying. You've learned to pray and you didn't even work at it! You're living, breathing Jesus Christ, for to you, "to live is Christ" (Philippians 1:21)!

I want you to see prayer in this way. Don't just think of it as something you do in a daily "quiet time." Don't only think of it as bowing your head and closing your eyes. Prayer is your constant communication with Christ, like a deep-sea diver breathing oxygen from above.

Then how do you keep your prayer life fresh? How do you keep the lines to God open and clear?

By a daily "quiet time"! And maybe by bowing your head and closing your eyes! Does that seem contradictory?

Jesus prayed continually, and 1 Thessalonians 5:17 says Christians must too—"without ceasing." That's "practicing God's presence," living in total communication with Him. He said "I am in the Father, and . . . the Father is in me" (John 14:10). There was the superimposing of their two lives, which made the

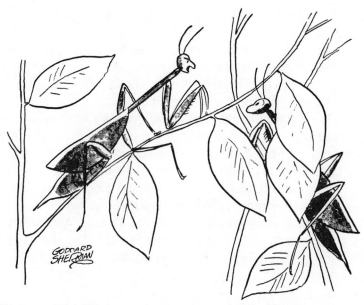

"I can't help it . . . I just don't feel like praying."

back-forth flow between the two unceasing. That's how it must be between you and God. It's the most important life habit you'll ever develop. I'm still working on it all the time.

But what fosters and strengthens it? Regular prayer times. I know that if I skip my own quiet time, I'm liable not to think of the Lord much otherwise! But if I have a good quality time of prayer in the morning, awareness of Him will probably be overshadowing me like a canopy all the rest of the day.

David wrote in Psalm 16:8, "I have set the Lord always before me." But he also said in Psalm 5:3, "Morning by morning, O Lord, you hear my voice; morning by morning I lay my requests before you and wait in expectation."

So the constant habit of prayer must be nurtured by structured prayer times. And structured prayer times must be learned; for them you need "ground rules," or a plan.

Are you with me?

Jesus' Suggested Outline for Your Prayers

Jesus' structured prayer life was evidently so attractive that His disciples said, "Lord, teach us to pray." And so He gave them a model; we call it The Lord's Prayer. The fact that He taught it to them twice and in not quite the same way tells us that it doesn't have to be slavishly repeated verbatim. It's a form, and it gives you the content of what good praying has in it. Put these elements in your prayer and you can't go wrong!

"Our Father in heaven." You can call Him that "through faith in Christ Jesus" (Galatians 3:26). What a precious relationship! You're in the family, a child of the Almighty. Not bad!

"But there are three Persons in the Trinity," you're saying. "Can't I pray to Jesus or to the Holy Spirit?" Well, I don't think He's going to "cuff you one" if you do, but Ephesians 2:18 gives you the pattern for normal prayer:

For through [Christ] we [all] have access to the Father by one Spirit.

1. You pray *through,* or in the name of, *the Lord Jesus Christ* (John 14:6).

2. You pray *to the Father* (Ephesians 3:14).

3. And you pray *by the enabling of the Holy Spirit* (Romans 8:26,27).

Now don't picture the Father far away in heaven, Christ somewhere halfway in between, and the Spirit inside of you helping you pray. All three are within you!

1 John 4:12 says God lives in you.

Colossians 1:27 says Christ is in you.

1 Corinthians 6:19 says the Holy Spirit is in you.

Yet *all three are in heaven!* The Lord's prayer addresses the "Father in heaven." Acts 1:11 says Jesus is in heaven And Revelation 14·13 says the Holy Spirit is in heaven

How do you figure it? It's good to think about it, but it's beyond us. So just kneel in humble adoration and pray. *"Hallowed be your name."* "O God, You are holy!" Always begin your prayer with worship! Look right into His face, and admire Him in all the ways you can. That's what they're doing in heaven (Revelation 4:8).

"Your kingdom come, Your will be done on earth as it is in heaven." Christian, live your prayer life and live *all* your life in the light of Jesus' sure return. He is coming bodily to this earth a second time (Acts 1:11) to set up His kingdom of justice and righteousness. The Bible ends with "Come, Lord Jesus,"—the opposition done away, and Jesus standing high and lofty over all. Lose yourself in the glory of the Big Picture!

Next you have requests. In the Lord's Prayer they're asking for three things: material supply, forgiveness of past sins, and avoidance of future sins.

"Give us this day our daily bread." Notice the prayer doesn't say "me" but "us." "Lord, this is what I want not only for myself but for my brothers and sisters in Christ." It's so easy for us to pray selfishly!

Here's a prayer of John Ward, M.P., dated 1727. It's come down to us word for word, but history has lost for us whether it's serious or satire:

> O Lord, thou knowest that I have nine houses in the city of London, and that I have lately purchased an estate in Essex. I beseech thee to preserve the two counties of Middlesex and Essex from fire and earthquakes. And as I have also a mortgage in Hertfordshire I beg thee also to have an eye of compassion on that county, and for the rest of the counties, thou mayest deal with them as thou mayest.
>
> O Lord, enable the banks to answer all their bills, and make all the debtors good men. Give prosperous voyage and safe return to the *Mermaid* sloop, because I have not insured it

Preserve me from thieves and housebreakers, and make all my servants so honest and faithful that they may always attend to my interests, and never cheat me out of my property night or day.

Or this prayer of a parent:

O Lord, do not let William grow up too quickly. May he make no decisions without consulting me first. Remind him constantly of all that he owes to his parents, and prevent him from growing too independent. And if it must be that he have a girl friend, let it be sweet little Cynthia Black.

No, don't just pray for you and yours!

About this prayer for bread. Don't "spiritualize" it; don't say it must mean spiritual food. I don't think that's what Jesus means here at all; He's being completely practical. To be an honest person you need to pray honestly about your *bread,* as the kids say—your money—even your *daily* bread. Enough for the day: the groceries, the insurance premium, the braces for your teeth (or your kid's teeth), school tuition . . . God's Word says, pray for bread.

I was baby-sitting our grandkids awhile back and I was putting little redheaded Mindy, age five, to bed. I tucked her in and said, "Well, let's have some prayer, Mindy." She folded her hands getting ready to pray, and she looked up at me and said, "You guys need any money?"

That's what you call confidence in God's ability to be practical.

"*Forgive us our debts.*" Pray often for forgiveness. It's one of your most important needs. Dr. Karl Menninger has said about the people in his psychiatric hospital, "If I could get my patients to believe that their sins were forgiven, 70 percent could be released in twenty-four hours " When we pray "forgive us our debts," or sins, there's tragedy, ruin, hell, and torment behind those words.

But in order to pray this prayer without hypocrisy Jesus says to say, "Forgive us our debts as *we also have forgiven our debtors.*" No way can we ask God to do for us what we won't do for others!

God's forgiveness is powerful and complete. It forever separates the sinner from his sins (Psalm 103:12). Believe that, accept it, rejoice in it—and seek to copy it! Forgive others the same way. In your heart completely separate the person from the sin you know about. What if the memory of it keeps popping up? Forgive seventy times seven!

Praying this way will keep your own life renewed; you'll stay cleansed in all your relationships. Hallelujah! "Lord, as far as I know I've forgiven everybody. Now forgive me."

"And lead us not into temptation, but deliver us from the evil one." Pray you'll avoid sin. "Lord, guide me away from situations that are too much for me to cope with. You know my Waterloos. You know my weaknesses."

Pray against your own natural inclinations to goof. Pray protectively. I try to do that. I know where I'm vulnerable!

So there's a pattern for your prayers. Call Him "Father," worship Him, pray for the fulfillment of His worldwide plans, and ask Him for things. Be reverent; be practical.

When Should You Have Prayer Times?

Probably the greatest advertisement and promotion for prayer is the praying Christ Himself. When you read through the Gospels (Matthew, Mark, Luke, and John, which recount His earthly life) you see that Jesus was a person of prayer.

Jesus prayed regularly. In Luke 5:15,16, at the beginning of His ministry when His popularity was high and His opposition low, Jesus often withdrew and prayed. He didn't wait for the "foxholes," the "pits." Neither must you!

But at the end of His ministry when His popularity was low and the opposition was high, Jesus was still praying. It was even His last act before being arrested (John 18:1–12).

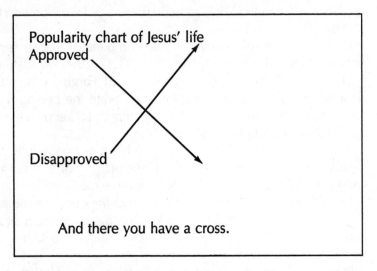

Popularity chart of Jesus' life
Approved

Disapproved

And there you have a cross.

When you're up, pray. When you're down, pray. Whatever your circumstances, pray. It will keep you steady, consistent, obedient.

Jesus prayed when He was preparing for something great: we find Him being baptized, in preparation for His three years of earthly ministry . . . *praying* (Luke 3:21).

Jesus prayed before making major decisions: we find Him the night before He chose His twelve apostles . . . *praying* (Luke 6:12,13).

Jesus prayed before strenuous activity: we find Him early in the morning while it was still dark . . . *praying* (Mark 1:35–39).

Jesus prayed after strenuous activity: we find Him following the feeding of the five thousand alone in the hills . . . *praying* (Mark 6:46).

Jesus prayed at ordinary times: like saying the blessing before a meal (Mark 6:41).

Jesus prayed in extraordinary times, too: as when He was hanging on the cross itself (Matthew 27:46).

He prayed, He prayed. It was His habit; it was His natural reflex. It was part of His very life; it was woven into His very being.

And that's what prayer must be for you and me.

How Should You Have Prayer Times?

Jesus prayed when He was full of words. The whole seventeenth chapter of John, He prayed long and intensely to His Father. Here prayer was royal battle.

Jesus prayed when He had no words at all. In Mark 7:34 He was healing a deaf man and He just "looked up to heaven." He glanced at God; that was the general idea. I don't know, maybe He rolled His eyes as if to say, *"Oi vay!* This guy is really bad, isn't he, Father."

Jesus prayed on occasion with great persistence. In the Garden of Gethsemane He was "deeply distressed and troubled." He had with Him the inner circle of His disciples, Peter, James, and John, and He asked them to intercede while He went a little distance and "fell to the ground" in groans of prayer.

Then He checked on His three friends (and found them *asleep!*) and went back and prayed some more. Again He returned to His sleeping colleagues and went back to prayer a third time. Hebrews 5:7, without doubt referring to this very time, says He "offered up prayers and petitions with loud cries and tears."

When was the last time you cried—not at the movies but in prayer? I'm amazed at the tremendous value God puts on our earnest persistence.

Jesus told a story in Luke 11 of a fellow knocking on his friend's door at midnight to ask him for bread because he'd run short; and the friend at first said no. Jesus had been teaching on prayer, and obviously the friend with bread is God.

And then Jesus says an incredible thing: "I tell you, though he will not get up and give him the bread *because he is his friend,* yet because of the man's *persistence* he will get up and give him as much as he needs" (italics mine).

Jesus says that in prayer, relationship is the right beginning—but *relationship is not enough.* God is trying to get us to *pray,* and only persistence will make Him answer.

Shocking? Luke 18:1–8 says the same thing.

Let's move in, then. Apparently God thinks this prayer matter is serious business.

A FORMULA FOR PRAYER THAT'S
HELPED ME: <u>ACTS</u>

Adoration: begin by worshiping Him. List the good things He is and does.

Confession: list your sins.

Thanksgiving: list your blessings.

Supplication: list what you want.

I find that He wants me to be very specific in all four areas. Sometimes I write out my prayers. Anne writes hers almost every day in her notebook.

I don't want you to think of prayer as a rigid formula—but oh, we need every help we can find to get us actually *praying*!

You see, we all have a chapel inside. God made us that way—with a chamber where we're to worship Him, where the Holy Spirit calls to us. Every person has one.

Some set up in their chapel an image of Buddha or some other god. Some put in a TV set, or the logo of their company; some worship that. Some put in a person: a wife or husband or kids, or themselves! St. Augustine prayed this: "Lord, thou hast made us for thyself, and our hearts are restless until they rest in thee."

In an interview on a radio program I was asked, "You've been in the ministry for a number of years now; what would you do differently if you could do it all over again?"

I had no trouble answering that! Right away I said, "I'd pray more. And I'd do all I could to get other people to pray more." James 4:2 says to us, *"You do not have, because you do not ask God."*

But there's this strange reluctance in us to pray. My mind wanders. Does yours too? I can't pray in my office very well. I pray, but then I see those letters over there . . . and I think, *Well, I'll stick to my praying* . . . and pretty soon I'm answering a letter! Or I think, *I've got to phone so-and-so.*

I'm jumpy, I'm fidgety. Maybe you don't have that problem but I do, I do. I have to take myself by the scruff of the neck and say, "Ortlund, you big sinner, pray! Go after God!" So I walk, I stand, I lift my hands to God, I bow my head, I get down on the floor, I do everything I can to help me really communicate with God.

And as I do, God moves in mighty ways, and fabulous changes come in my life, and remarkable answers to my prayers.

No One Else Can Pray for You

This is a true story. A minister was once asked to offer the customary opening prayer at the New York Legislature, and he went to the podium and said, "I will not pray for you! There are certain things a man has to do for himself. He must blow his own nose, make his own love, and pray his own prayers. Pray yourselves."

Well, I think God can use us sometimes to pray on behalf of others, but basically he was right. You should not rely on the prayers of others. Even a newborn baby has to take his own milk.

Ask the Holy Spirit right now to start saturating your life with prayer—both the habitual breathings of unceasing prayer to

God, and regular, structured prayer times as well. Without these you'll become as phony as a three-dollar bill!

Nobody loves a good time more than I do. I really have a "ball" in life. But when I look back and ask myself what are the most exhilarating and satisfying and memorable times I've ever had, I'll tell you what I think of.

I remember when my mother knelt beside me at the front of our church and I received Jesus as my Savior.

I remember the Sunday mornings when Dad gathered the family around the breakfast table and read the Bible and prayed for us.

I remember when my big brother was going off to war and all the family was gathered in the living room, and a dear friend prayed.

I think of the times Anne and I have, as we're driving in the car or as we're wrapped in each other's arms, and we pray together. The happiest times, the times we love each other most, are right then.

I think of times when we've been around the dining table with our children, or in one of our living rooms with the grandchildren too, and we all just praise the Lord together. Even the little kids! Happy times! Glory, glory! Because of prayer times like these my life is fulfilled.

And I think of kneeling before the Father in small support groups of dear Christian brothers and sisters, and enjoying each other's victories, or crying to God together over each other's kids. . . .

And I love church prayer services that are really for prayer. I think of Edward L. Johnson, a member of a church I served and also a man very important in our country's finances. How seriously he took his commitment to pray! I remember his phoning me long distance on a Wednesday to explain that he was in Washington and would have to miss prayer meeting that evening.

I think of multitudes of times when I've grabbed hands with someone struggling with disappointments or sins, and we've prayed together. How healing those times are, how fulfilling!

The greatest experiences of life are prayer experiences. Be hungry for them. Go after them. Carve them out in your life—praying alone, praying with others.

I'll never forget going to the First Baptist Church in Dallas—a huge church, glorious in red carpet. Here came the pastor, Dr. Criswell, and others who were going to take part and they didn't sit down; they dropped to their knees. And in came the deacons and their wives, up to the altar rail at the front of the church and they dropped to their knees too. No one said anything; they simply came and they prayed. There was glory in that sanctuary. "My house is to be a house of prayer," said Jesus. It was a holy time in my own heart.

And the most wonderful moments of all for me have been my daily meetings with God. I haven't always felt a lot at the time, but I've told God I love Him, and reviewed my schedule with Him, and committed my life to Him again. . . .

Do You Pray?

You've been a Christian for a while now. Christian, do you pray? I want to pray more. I'm ashamed to tell you I'm not a great man of prayer, but I want to be. Prayer is so much like the weather, isn't it; we discuss it and don't do anything about it!

Listen, answer this in your own heart. Do you pray? Not do you say your prayers or do you go to church. You see, other people can tell when you're going to church or when you're studying your Bible or when you're doing this or that, but only you and God know if you really pray. Oh, you can bow your head and close your eyes; many a time I've had my head bowed in church when someone else was leading in prayer, but I didn't pray. Actually, I was checking out my shoes or thinking about what I would say when the prayer was over.

Great men of God may be Presbyterians or Pentecostalists; they may be Calvinists or Arminians—but those who walk with God are men and women of prayer. Great experiences given by

God—times of revival and renewal—may have lots of ingredients, but they're always times of prayer.

Do you pray? You may have convictions and feelings about the Christian life; you may be learning more about doctrine and this is important, but do you pray? Do you really pray? Your Christian life will never work unless you pray.

You want to be a mature and stable Christian. You want to be a happy, fulfilled person. Then pray! Ordinary, powerless Christians are prayerless. It's the way to be like everybody else. Where is another Elijah—"a man just like us" who prevailed in prayer? Be persistent in prayer; Christian, go hard after God.

You have a Father who cares for you. You must pray. Seek His face. Love Him. Adore Him. Call out to Him. Tell Him what's going on. Prayer is the simplest of all acts. You can do it anywhere at any time under any conditions.

> "No prayer, no power.
> Little prayer, little power.
> Much prayer, much power!"
> —Peter Deyneka

God wants to be totally involved in your life as a Christian, from moment to moment to moment. You mustn't ever move Him out of your field of action and into the bleachers as a spectator. Not ever. Not for one minute.

The only glory you'll ever know is the glory that comes from putting God in the center where the action is, and everything else on the sidelines.

Thank You, Lord, for stirring our minds to pray, mine the writer and this one, the reader. Launch us both by Your Spirit, we beseech You, into a great adventure of obedience

Lord, teach me to pray (Luke 11:1). Would You let me learn the habit of praying *always* by learning to pray *regularly*?

As You help me, I will seek to pray

On Sundays at _____

On Mondays at _____

On Tuesdays at _____

On Wednesdays at _____

On Thursdays at _____

On Fridays at _____

On Saturdays at _____

Questions for Review

1. Why is it so important to maintain a regular time of prayer each day?
2. Did Jesus' prayer life seem to follow any particular pattern? Name at least four instances when He prayed; tell why His prayers at such times were significant.
3. Repeat the "ACTS" formula for prayer. Define each of the four elements

FOUR

Lord, I Need to Be Constantly Sure I'm Yours

For background, first read 1 John 3:1—5:13

I was a young sailor in the U.S. Navy, on shore leave in New York City, "doing the town" with a buddy. He was a Christian and so was I. But instead of having fun seeing the sights of New York, we were walking block after block engrossed in a heated argument!

Dave said, "Ray, every Christian should always know he's a Christian forever!"

I said, "That's presumptuous. What if you kill somebody? Do you think God's going to say, 'It's okay, Dave, I won't notice that; I like you anyway, so come on into heaven'?"

Dave argued, "Anybody who really understands God's fabu-

49

lous salvation isn't going to want to kill somebody. But you're off the point. If a big sin could make you a dropout and a little sin wouldn't, how are you going to decide which one's big enough to disqualify you?"

I said, "That's why you try to live a good Christian life."

Dave jeered, "So you run scared. God's up there with a big stick, and you never know when He's going to go WHAMMO."

I objected, "That's not fair! He's a God of love!"

Said Dave: "How loving? A little bit? A lot? When will He stop loving you, if His love is based on your performance? Is eternal life really eternal, or are you on probation until the end?"

Around and around we went, and actually what we said was more important to me than seeing New York. I wanted to believe him.

I'd been raised in a warm, fervent family and church, but I never believed I could have assurance about my standing with God. So I was never quite certain that I'd made it into permanence with Jesus Christ. I was never really sure that He'd totally accepted me, mars, scars, and all.

In some ways I was miserable! I didn't know which sin I might commit that would make God say, "Okay, that's it." And He'd push me out the door and say, "When you've gotten your act together you can come back in."

I "went forward" at a lot of altar calls, trying to stay on His good side.

I remember that day in New York when finally in exasperation Dave crossed the street. From the opposite curb he called to me, "On this side of the street is confidence. On this side you see that salvation isn't a joint project, partly yours and partly God's. Over here you know that your salvation rests totally on His wonderful power to keep you. On this side you rely on Him and not yourself.

"Ray, why don't you cross over?"

I'll never forget it I crossed

A. Four Reasons Some People Aren't Sure They're Christians

1. *Because they're not Christians!* "This is how you can recognize the Spirit of God: Every spirit that acknowledges that Jesus Christ has come in the flesh is from God, but every spirit that does not acknowledge Jesus is not from God. This is the spirit of the antichrist, which you have heard is coming and even now is already in the world" (1 John 4:2,3).

The letter of 1 John is not only written to assure believers that they have eternal life—it's also to assure unbelievers that they don't. John wants to destroy false security, and he says that everything hinges on whether you accept Jesus.

It isn't how good you are. It isn't whether you go to church or try to live clean.

The first series of meetings I ever preached for was in Carlisle, Pennsylvania, at a church where the gospel wasn't really taught with assurance, and therefore wasn't really taught clearly.

It was wonderful—the Spirit of God came upon those meetings. I gave invitations to accept Jesus night after night, and a lot of people did.

One young woman who openly received Christ was a Sunday school teacher and a key worker in the church; the pastor's wife had a fit. "You're all right!" she insisted. "You don't need to do this; there's nothing the matter with you!" But that Sunday school teacher clearly saw the facts of the gospel for the first time that night. And receiving the message with joy and assurance of what God had done for her, she was motivated for life! Today she is one of the outstanding Bible teachers of that city.

Assurance is comforting and wonderful—but she had no right to have assurance until she had confessed her personal trust in Jesus Christ.

Sincerity is not enough! You can have a cold and sincerely take the wrong medicine and die. The point is not how sincere you are. In John 14:6 Jesus proclaimed, "I am the way—and the truth, and the life. No one comes to the Father except through me." Only Jesus Christ can save you.

Martin Luther had been a priest for years when for the first time he saw that his own works could never save him, but that trusting in the pure mercy and grace of Christ alone could and would. Then he wrote:

By the Spirit of God I understood the words "the just shall live by faith." I felt born again. Like a new man I entered through the open doors into the very paradise of God.

Martin Luther's confidence in the true gospel was so explosive and revolutionary that he became the father of modern day Protestantism.

2. *Because they're waiting for lightning to strike.* They're waiting for some super experience, some big "whammy" from God.

They have read about the Apostle Paul in Acts 9. Here he was, traveling on a road to Damascus, when a light from heaven blinded him and struck him down, and the voice of Christ spoke to him audibly. That's quite an experience! Somebody answered a person who was waiting for Paul's experience, "Man, when God was after the Apostle Paul, He was stalking big game! God used His big guns!"

Or think of the Philippian jailer. He got converted the night a tremendous earthquake released all his prisoners. But people who use his story in Acts 16:23–34 as an example need to read a few verses right before that which tell how Lydia became a Christian: "The Lord opened her heart." That was it. No huge experience, no fireworks, just a quiet conversion.

God doesn't run out of ideas on how to bring people to Himself. Sometimes it may be an explosion. Sometimes it's the way the Christmas hymn tells it:

How silently, how silently
The wondrous gift is giv'n!
So God imparts to human hearts

The blessings of His heaven.
No ear may hear His coming,
But in this world of sin
Where meek souls will receive Him still,
The dear Christ enters in.

Never mind *how* Christ comes to you. Just make sure *that* He's come.

3. *Because they don't know they can be sure.* If you ask them if they're Christians they say, "I hope so. I want to be."

Maybe you truly believe in Jesus, but as you're reading this you're saying (as I used to say as a young Christian) "I really don't know for sure!" Listen, God loves you very much, and He doesn't want you to live in a no-man's-land of wondering whether you're in or out.

Do you lack what Hebrews 10:22 calls "the full assurance of faith"? Paul wrote in 2 Timothy 1:12, "I know whom I have believed, and am convinced that he is able to guard what I have entrusted to him for that day." God wants you to enjoy that same wonderful reliance on His ability to hold you fast.

Another story about a Christian "heavy." John Wesley was an ordained priest in the Church of England, a devout high churchman and a brilliant scholar. He believed in his church's creed, he was full of good works—all that, but he was aware of something lacking inside.

He went from England to America to be a missionary in Georgia, and there he came in contact with Moravians. They did things quite differently from him and he wasn't really sure whether they were right or not, but he made an appointment with one of their leaders, a Mr. Spangenberg.

This godly older man asked him, "Do you know that Jesus Christ is the Son of God?"

John answered, "I know that He is the Savior of the world."

"True, but has He saved you?"

"Well, I hope so. He died to save me."

So the question was put in Wesley's mind. Later he returned to London, still unsure, until his experience when attending a Moravian meeting. He tells about it himself:

In the evening I went very unwillingly to a Society in Aldersgate Street, where one was reading Luther's preface to the Epistle to the Romans. About a quarter before nine, while he was describing the change which God works in hearts through faith in Christ, I felt my heart strangely warmed. I felt I did trust in Christ, Christ alone, for salvation; and an assurance was given me that he had taken away *my* sin, even mine—and saved me from the law of sin and death.

Later someone wrote about John Wesley, "He was instantly, absolutely changed from being a dull and anxious soul, turning here and there for blessing that seemed to elude him, into a happy, confident man" who began at once a mission that was to change the face of England and alter the whole turn of history.

4. *Because they may simply be in a time of depression.* One time I tried to comfort a young Christian I know very well, but she was in a "down" time and there was no comforting her. All she could say was, "I don't know if God is there or not. I just don't know anything." Well, He still loved her anyway, but sometimes to God's own, genuine people, reality is just not reality.

I remember a world-famous Bible teacher saying to me when he was depressed, "Ray, I don't even know if I'm a Christian." The great Charles Spurgeon occasionally went into black moods and would say the same thing.

Don't believe your emotions; believe God! And yet if you ever do doubt—even "if we are faithless, he will remain faithful, for he cannot disown himself" (2 Timothy 2:13).

A new Christian said once, "I'm afraid I'll slip through His fingers." And somebody who understood the truth of the body of Christ answered, "My friend, you *are* one of His fingers!"

There will be times in your life when you need to know the *facts* of your salvation, when you don't *feel* anything at all.

B. Permanent Acts of God Upon Your Life the Moment You Received Jesus Christ:

1. You were born of the Spirit, given new life, born from above (John 3:8).

2. You were baptized into the body of Christ (1 Corinthians 12:13). There is no water in this baptism. It simply means you were thrust into Christ, identified totally with Him in the family of God.

3. You were sealed by the Holy Spirit of God (Ephesians 1:13,14). You were marked by God with the seal of His Spirit, sort of the way letters used to be sealed with wax so that they were the possession of one person only. You were sealed to be God's—"to the praise of his glory."

"I seem to irritate everyone."

Reprinted with permission from The Saturday Evening Post Society, a division of the BFL & MS, Inc. © 1982.

4. You were redeemed (1 Peter 1:18,19).

5. You were totally forgiven (Colossians 2:13,14).

6. You were blessed with every spiritual blessing in Christ (Ephesians 1:3).

7. You were adopted by God, to receive a Father-child relationship (Romans 8:15,16).

8. You were made co-heirs with Christ, to share now in His sufferings and afterward in His glory (Romans 8:17).

9. You were raised up with Christ and seated with Him in heavenly realms (Ephesians 2:6).

And on and on! The New Testament lists thirty-three different things that happen to a believer instantly, permanently, when he accepts Christ. Why don't you look for them?

A new baby born into this world has no idea what's happening to him. He could spend the rest of his life becoming an important obstetrician-gynecologist and hardly begin to understand all that happened to him when he was born.

So with the new baby Christian. The more you study God's Word and learn all the fabulous things He's done for you, the more your assurance, your confidence in Him will grow.

You live in a world that's full of change. Governments are changing; lifestyles, ideas about morals, continually go through change. But John wants you to enter into a world of Christian certainty. "I write these things to you who believe in the name of the Son of God so that you may know that you have eternal life" (1 John 5:13).

C. Three-Way Test by Which You May Know That You Have Eternal Life

Test 1, the intellectual test: Do you believe that Jesus is the Christ? Yes or no _____

"Everyone who believes that Jesus is the Christ is born of God" (1 John 5:1).

This was important in the days of the early church, just as it is today. There were a lot of heresies floating around then, too. One that particularly concerned John was championed by a fellow named Cerinthus.

The early church historian Irenaeus tells a story of John's unplanned confrontation with Cerinthus. John was going to bathe in the public bathhouse in Ephesus, and, says Irenaeus, "perceiving Cerinthus within, he rushed out of the bathhouse without bathing, exclaiming, 'Let us fly! Lest even the bathhouse fall down! Cerinthus is within, the enemy of truth!' "

(We hope when he ran out he still had something on.)

Then Irenaeus gives the reason John got so excited. He says Cerinthus represented Jesus as not being born of a virgin but as simply the human son of Joseph and Mary. He taught that Jesus was "more righteous, prudent, and wise than other men," but that the divine nature (he called this *the Christ*) came upon him only temporarily. In his words he said, "Moreover, after Jesus' baptism Christ descended on him in the form of a dove from the supreme ruler—that then he proclaimed the unknown Father. Then he performed miracles. . . .

"But at last the Christ departed from Jesus, when Jesus went to suffer and to die and rise again, while the Christ remained impassible [unaffected] by it all, inasmuch as he was a spiritual being."

"Heresy! heresy!" cried John. "I won't even go into a bathhouse with anyone who says that! You can't have a part-time Christ! You must believe that 'Jesus Christ has come in the flesh' (1 John 4:2). If you don't, you're not of God."

Again 1 John 5:1 says: "Everyone who believes that Jesus is the Christ is born of God."

Christian, there's a lot of doctrinal mushiness these days. Anything goes. But don't be a fuzzy thinker. Study to get assurance of God's truths. Open your eyes! Avoid false teachers. That's terribly important. Make sure you understand the gospel intellectually.

Test 2, the spiritual or the inward test: Do you have the witness, or the inner testimony of God's Spirit that you are His child? Yes or no _____

1 John 5:9,10 says, "We accept man's testimony, but God's testimony is greater because it is the testimony of God, which he has given about his Son. Anyone who believes in the Son of God has this testimony in his heart."

People accept each other's testimony without too much difficulty. I went with a friend recently to a car auction. I want to tell you, when the auctioneer was rattling off prices you'd better not scratch your nose; you might have yourself a new car! That auctioneer did all his business on the testimony of men—even the slightest wiggle. I understand the stock market works the same way.

John says if we rely on the testimony of men, the testimony of God is greater. And what is that testimony? It's the testimony of His Spirit within your heart.

Back in my Navy days there was a guy I loved to pray with: a black Christian who was so fun and natural. This fellow would sit on the back row in the chapel aboard ship, and when the chaplain would say something he agreed with, he'd lean back in his chair and exclaim, "Truth indeed, truth indeed!"

That's what the Holy Spirit does for you. When you hear the truth of God His Spirit within you says, "That's right! Truth indeed. You are a true child of God."

Test 3, the relational test: Do you love your fellow Christians? Yes or no _____

"Dear friends, if our hearts do not condemn us, we have confidence before God. . . . And this is his command: to believe in the name of his Son, Jesus Christ, and to love one another as he commanded us" (1 John 3:21,23).

"We know that we have passed from death to life, because we love our brothers. Anyone who does not love remains in death" (1 John 3:14).

He doesn't say "because we love some of our brothers." Not just "the beautiful people." Not just the ones who've treated you well. We love our brothers—the whole church of God. It's

"We may as well go home. It's obvious that this meeting isn't going to settle anything."

Drawing by Booth; © 1979 The New Yorker Magazine, Inc.

a serious test. I think there are those who believe the right doctrine, and they may even feel good things, but they fail Test 3. 2 Corinthians 13:5 would say, "Examine yourselves to see whether you are in the faith; test yourselves. Do you not realize that Christ Jesus is in you—unless, of course, you fail the test?"

There are always odd people, "strangies," in the church of God. God puts them there to stretch our hearts to incorporate them all in love. And there are always those who in the past have injured us. How do you handle them?

Do names or faces pop into memory right now? If you are a genuine child of God, His Spirit nevertheless is prompting you quickly to make things right. "If you . . . remember that your brother has something against you . . . first go and be reconciled to your brother" (Matthew 5:23,24).

I've laughed with other Christians when they've said, "The church is like Noah's ark. You couldn't stand the stink inside if the storm outside weren't so bad!" But as you look at 1 John 3:14, at least one reason for the "stink inside" becomes apparent: there must be some church members who aren't genuine Christians.

Make this vow to God right now, sign your name to it, and write the date:
"God helping me, I will remain constantly sure all my life that I am a Christian, because I seek to stay constantly in fellowship with every believer I know."

Name _____

Date _____

Let your heart stretch and grow to love more and more Christians, and never stop stretching and growing! Love "everyone who believes that Jesus is the Christ . . . born of God" (1 John 5:1), whether he—

Wears robes, swings incense, and chants;

Worships in a simple storefront and disdains those who do the above;

Is white, black, brown, or yellow;

Is charismatic or anticharismatic;

Worships on Saturday, Sunday, or another day;

Has one idea or another about particulars of Christ's return;

Belongs to this council or that denomination or none at all;

Baptizes three times forward or once backward or doesn't even dunk. . . .

Love them all! If anyone starts to spoil you by whispering suspicions about this group or that person, don't listen. Some "old Christians" are wise about Christ, but some are wise about all the latest dirt on everybody. Avoid all that!

I think it was Wesley who said, "I want the whole world for my parish; I want the whole Bible for my book; I want the whole

Christ for my Savior; and I want the whole church for my fellowship!''

Did you pass all three tests? Then rejoice! You're a true Christian forever. If you ever have a time of doubting again, go back and check the FOUR REASONS. You'll find you can check off 1, 2, and probably 3. If your problem is reason 4, memorize and rely upon 2 Timothy 2:13: "If we are faithless, he will remain faithful, for he cannot disown himself.''

Questions for Review

1. Is it possible to be sure you are saved?
2. What are four reasons a person may not be sure?
3. Look again at the Three-Way Test. Tell or write out in your own words the meaning of each

FIVE

Lord, I Want to Understand the Bible

For background, first read Psalm 19:7–11

Suppose a husband had to be separated from his wife for two whole years. He had to go on a special secret mission that would keep him overseas without communication for that long, long time!

He'd really prepare. He'd probably spend a lot of time writing out everything he could think of that he wanted to say to his wife and family. Part of it would be a love letter! Part of it would be instructions about the finances, the kids' schooling, possible medical problems, upkeep of the house and car, what to do in case of this or that. . . .

Now suppose when he left, the wife stuck the letter in her

desk saying, "Gotta read that someday." And once in a while she'd get it out and read a snatch or two; but the whole two years she never read it wholly and thoroughly, so she never really knew well what he had in mind.

Besides that, with the letter stuck away in the desk drawer, she thought of him less and less, and by the time he got back she was having a full-blown affair with another fellow.

The Bible is God's love letter-instruction book to you. He wrote it with great care over a long period of time, and it gives you everything you need to stay spiritually renewed until He comes back.

Don't stick it away somewhere!

Don't read it in periodic snatches!

He meant it *all* for us, and every word's important.

But it seems really long! How are you going to master the whole thing? Well, if He'd felt it should have been shorter, He'd have made it so. We can trust Him about that.

Take the Bible Seriously

I was brought up in a loving and wonderful relationship to the Bible. I was taught to respect it. I went to Sunday school from the time I can remember.

Then, as you know, I went into the Navy—and what joining the Navy really means is that brother, you've come to "sink or swim" time. And I was about to sink! I remember one night I went out on the drill field. I had with me my little New Testament that the church had given me, and I said, "Lord, I'm not going to make it! You've got to help me."

In His kind grace (He's always ready to meet you at those times) he sent me to Oakland, California, where I went into town and got into a fellowship of people in a church, and there I met some Navigators. Navigators is a ministry that disciples young believers and gets them going in God's Word. One fellow particularly took me on

I'll never forget the first night I had dinner at his home. He said, "Ray, how long have you known the Lord?"

I said, "I really don't know. Since I was a little kid, anyway."

He said, "Tell me what you know about the Bible and about the Christian life."

I said, "Well, I memorized Psalm One and the Twenty-third Psalm, and I know John 3:16 and probably a few other verses like that. . . ." I was sort of scratching around.

He had a fit! He said, "You mean to tell me you're out there in the world where they're apt to chew you up and spit you out, and you don't have any more of the Bible in you than *that*?"

So I found out I needed to get with the program. He took me under his wing, this Navigator. I'll be thankful for him till the day I die. He made me memorize three verses a week; he taught me to analyze chapters; he put pressure on me. He sort of let me know that any week I came up short I'd be a weak cop-out who should be ashamed of himself. But the pressure also said he cared for me and wanted terribly for me to become a man of God.

I wish I could become that Navigator to you, only maybe a bit more gentle! The Bible gives you God's view of life, of creation, of good and evil, of time and eternity, and His purposes for the whole world and for you. You learn in the Bible what you can't find out any other place. Let it become your food and drink. Learn to live it and breathe it.

When you hear preaching, bring a looseleaf notebook and take full notes, so before long you can pass them on to others.[5] If you can, become a regular student of some of the good radio Bible teachers; listen to tapes, read books, get into a Bible class. Maybe take a correspondence course from Moody Bible Institute in Chicago or somewhere. The world is full of opportunities to get that Book of Books inside of you.

But what's the whole thing about? In a certain building in Washington, D.C., there's a plaque on the wall. It's the U.S. Constitution, engraved in copper plate. When you look closely you read the words of the Constitution. But when you step back, at a distance you see the face of George Washington.

It's that way with the Bible. Look closely, and read what it says. Step back, and you see Christ.

We call it the Word of God, and it absolutely is, but it's the word of men too. It's phenomenal! Unlike any other book, it's both human and divine. 2 Peter 1:20,21 says that it was written by men, and yet not by their own interpretation; they "spoke from God as they were carried along by the Holy Spirit."

One of the Old Testament writers, David, spoke of writing "because the hand of the Lord was upon" him (1 Chronicles 28:19). And get this: 1 Peter 1:10,11 says the writers "searched intently and with the greatest care," trying to find out what the Spirit meant in the words He had them write down!

Here it is—a plain, open book for anyone to read. *And yet:* the Bible contains both the open and the hidden, the public and the secret. On the one hand it's about real people and places—history for any historian to check. And it has a public message, clear and complete, to lead any honest reader into an eternal relationship with God through Jesus Christ.

On the other hand, it has depths, significances, characteristics, and proofs of supernaturalness which it reveals only to those with Spirit-led hearts.

Two Ways to Read the Bible

A. Read the Bible as a Careful Student

Spend your life studying the Bible in every open, logical way you can.

1. Look for its most flat-out, obvious meanings.
2. See its sections.
3. Study to whom it was written.
4. See by whom it was written.

5. Study under what circumstances it was written, and for what purpose.

Become grounded and established in it as Ephesians 1:17–19 tells you. For this, many of the finest scholars of twenty centuries have applied their minds and spent their lives. You join a noble bunch!

You'll discover it's one book but it contains sixty-six books, written by about forty authors over a period of about 1600 years.

You'll discover it's got two "testaments"—the Old Testament with thirty-nine books in it, and the New Testament with twenty-seven. Testaments are covenants or "deals" that God made with people. A testament (like part of a will) is a solemn oath, something you promise other people.

The Old Testament	The New Testament
Is a record of a *nation*, the Jews.	Is the record of the *church*, of all ages and peoples.
Concerns *earthly* people elected by God through Abraham.	Concerns *spiritual* people elected by God through Christ.
Tells about a covenant built on *law*, laying out God's requirements for human righteousness.	Tells about a covenant built on *grace* (God's kindness without rules and regulations).
Centers in *Moses*, through whom the law was given.	Centers in *Jesus Christ*, who perfectly fulfilled all God's requirements for righteousness.

The Old Covenant lays out "God's requirements for human righteousness."

That sounds a little hopeless, right? God tested the Jews on the law. He did it to show that imposing laws on people doesn't work! He showed the whole world that even under the best of conditions (in a land "flowing with milk and honey") nobody's good enough to come up to His perfect standard of righteousness.

But always God built hope into them: Part of His Old Testament "deal" was that He would soon send Christ to do what the law couldn't—to save people from their sins and make them truly good.

And He did—in Jesus. So God's new "deal" is, "Forget the law; forget the Jews as special. The grand experiment is over; the test is finished. Now everyone's on equal footing again; and your only, your universal requirement is to accept Jesus Christ's death as the payment of punishment for your personal sins, and I'll reckon you totally righteous and perfect in my holy eyes" (*see* Romans 3:21–24).

Wonderful—but wait! God made some special promises to the Jews in His Old Covenant. Does the New Covenant wipe all that out? No, in Psalm 89:34 God says, "I will not violate my covenant or alter what my lips have uttered."

So the New Testament's a double deal: It says that "Christ has come" and it also says, "Christ is coming again!" And the Second Coming will incorporate the fulfilling of all the promises, not only for the church, but also the old covenant promises for the Jews, reassembled and happy in their land again. "Such a deal!"

Now look at the table of contents in the front of your Bible. It lists the books in the Old and New Testaments, but what it doesn't say is that you can divide the Testaments into three sections each:

The Old Testament	The New Testament
History: Genesis to Esther	History: Matthew to Acts
Experience: Job to Song of Solomon	Experience: Romans to Jude
Prophecy: Isaiah to Malachi	Prophecy: Revelation

Take your Bible and put your fingers in the Old Testament history section—from Genesis to Esther. For the *story* of the Old

Testament, this is it. This completes the tale—from creation through God's choosing the Jews, giving them the law and their land, watching them fall into sin, and scattering them in disgrace over the world, as Esther describes it at the end.

Hang onto this section, and put your fingers around the New Testament history section, Matthew through Acts. Skinny, isn't it? Well, after that sad Old Testament ending you've got four hundred silent years when God didn't move people to write anything at all; and then Matthew picks up the story and describes the arrival of God's Christ, come to rescue and deliver. The Gospels—Matthew, Mark, Luke, and John—recount His life, death, and resurrection from their four viewpoints, and Acts tells how believers in Him carried on after His return to heaven.

Then what are all the rest of the pages you're not pinching between your fingers? Enormous appendages to the stories. The Old Testament appendage there on your left includes poetry books (you're going to *live* in the Psalms before long) and prophecy books. The New Testament appendage is mostly letters written to the churches that sprang up in the first century—plus Revelation, one final book of prophecy about the future. (It's amazing.)

The Bible needs to be your friend. Turn the pages; pray that you'll begin to understand deeply the precious thing you're holding.

Ask the Lord who could be in a small group with you—others who are also hungry to get hold of this Word of God. Then dig into it together, and memorize the titles of the books in order and say them to each other until you've got them down cold.

And get some tools you'll need over the years for study: a concordance, perhaps *The Ryrie Study Bible,* a Bible dictionary, *Halley's Bible Handbook,* the *Wycliffe Bible Commentary.* These are a few aids to understanding what you're reading.

	History Books	Events and People	Approximate Dates	Poetry, prophecy books and letters all fit somewhere into the books of history
Old Testament	Genesis 1	Creation		Poetry book: Job, maybe written before Flood
	Genesis 6 ff	Flood		
	Genesis 12 thru Deuteronomy	Beginning of Jewish history: Abraham through Moses	2000 B.C.	
	Joshua thru Ruth	Jews enter and settle their land	1500 B.C.	
	1,2 Samuel, 1 Kings 1–11 (repeat 1 Chron. 1–2 Chron. 9)	Kings Saul, David, Solomon	1000 B.C.	Poetry books Psalms through Song of Solomon
	1 Kings 12–22 (repeat 2 Chron. 10–35)	Spiritual decline and split into two kingdoms (Israel, 10 tribes; Judah, 2 tribes)	1000 B.C. to 600 B.C.	Prophecy books for warning: Isaiah, Jeremiah, and Hosea through Zephaniah

	Books	Events	Dates	Notes
	2 Kings 24, 25 and 2 Chron. 36, Ezra, Nehemiah, Esther	Israel, then Judah carried off into exile	600 B.C. to 400 B.C.	Poetry book of Lamentations. Prophecy books written during exile: Ezekiel, Daniel, Haggai, Zechariah, Malachi
			400 years of silence before beginning of New Testament	
New Testament	Matthew, Mark, Luke, John	Jesus' birth, life, death, resurrection	7 B.C. to A.D. 30	
	Acts	Jesus' ascension, birth and development of early church	A.D. 30 to A.D. 66	Letters: Romans through Jude
			A.D. 96	Prophecy book: Revelation

B. Read the Bible Devotionally

We said you need to read the Bible according to logical rules for its open, obvious meanings. But there's another way you also need to read it, and that's devotionally.

By that I mean, you need to read it expecting God's Spirit to speak to you and you alone in that moment. The Bible must challenge your mind, and don't shortchange that! But it must also nourish your heart. This is how God quietly shapes your personality, your humility, your zeal, your devotion. This is how He guides you and encourages you. This is how you grow in Christ-likeness and stay new and fresh all your life.

I was just a young guy in the ministry who'd hardly traveled anywhere when I was attending a conference at Glen Eyrie, Colorado. And one afternoon I walked out by myself and sat down on a rock and began to read my Bible. As sure as I'm telling you, God spoke to me that day through Acts 1:8. He lifted me right out of its 33 A.D. context and said to me, "Ray Ortlund, you'll receive power when the Holy Spirit comes upon you, and you'll be My witness to the ends of the earth."

I'd never had a ministry anywhere but in two local churches. It seemed such an enormous promise I was embarrassed about it, and I didn't even tell Anne for a few months. When I finally did, she bought a big map for my wall, to put gummed stickers on as God used me around the world. Amazing—that map is full of stickers now, on every world continent except Antarctica. And God has been wonderfully faithful to let me see revival particularly in Vietnam, Peru, Ecuador, Colombia, Afghanistan, Nigeria, and several places in the United States.

I remember another time when I was almost too discouraged to go on in a certain pastorate. And the moment it hit me the most deeply, I was across town late at night, having just visited someone in the hospital.

I remember I parked the car on a city street, got out and opened my Bible under a streetlight and said, "God, I'm not going on until You speak to me." And that night He gave me that wonderful Twenty-seventh Psalm, with its closing words:

I am still confident of this: I will see the goodness of the Lord in the land of the living. Wait for the Lord; be strong and take heart and wait for the Lord.

With those words He encouraged me to "hang in there," and it all worked out fine. God renewed me!

This doesn't mean the Bible is magic. Don't be superstitious in the way you read it. Some people get really "buggy" in their use of the Bible—like the fellow who decided he would find out what God wanted him to do, so he took his Bible, opened it at random and stuck his finger on a verse. It said, "Judas went out and hanged himself."

How depressing, he thought, and his finger stabbed again. This time the verse said, "Go thou and do likewise."

Now he was scared. He thought, *That's gotta be wrong; I'll try it again.* He opened to another place and it said, "What thou doest, do quickly."

Don't fool with the Bible! Expect to handle it in logical, objective, consistent ways. But then expect it also to become God's voice to you in unexpected ways—which only His Spirit within will discern for your own heart.

On the margins of my Bible I have written responses to God. These are sometimes pleas to God to fulfill a promise in my life such as Isaiah 42:9: "See, the former things have taken place, and the new things I declare; before they spring into being I announce them to you." I wrote beside that verse in a recent time when I needed guidance, "Lord, declare your 'new thing' to me and Anne. Show us the way to go."

Besides Proverbs 18:22, "He who finds a wife finds what is good and receives favor from the Lord," I recently wrote, "Thanks for your favor in giving me Anne. What 'good' she is to me!"

I was looking for guidance one day and I read, "Yet I am

always with you; you hold me by my right hand. You guide me with your counsel" (Psalm 73:23,24). I wrote beside that, "Thank You, Lord; You will be true to Your Word, I know."

This Fabulous Book You're Holding

Do you understand what it means to have it in your hand? In all history, you're one of the recent few.

Through the B.C. years the only way Jews could hear the Old Testament was to go to the temple, or later to the synagogues, and hear someone read from it. After Christ, believers would gather in a home or later a church and hear a piece of the New Testament read.

Through all those centuries the Bible was hand copied, very carefully. The letters were counted across the page—up and down and across to make sure nothing was added or subtracted with each new copy. But these hand-copied Scriptures were rare—and you might travel a long way to find one and hear it read in public.

It was not until A.D. 1456 that the first book was ever printed with movable type—and it was the Bible! Fabulous breakthrough! But even then very few had a Bible, and few could read it if they had it.

The centuries had passed, and still there are people in parts of the world who long for Bibles and have none, or have only a few treasured pages. . . .

But *here you are!* And at your disposal are a great number of delicately different English translations—to ponder and compare and muse over personally and hear God speak from. Just for you.

Earlier Christians, and believers overseas today, would give their eyeteeth . . . ! Pray with Psalm 119:18, "Open my eyes, that I may see wonderful things in your law"!

You can read anywhere in God's Word. Take a section each

day, and go after the main purpose of what it's saying. Ask yourself:

1. What you learn there about God the Father.
2. What you learn about God the Son.
3. What you learn about God the Holy Spirit.
4. What command in it you need to obey.
5. What example you need to follow.
6. What error you need to avoid.
7. What promise you can claim.

You can do this alone or in little groups, and dig into great treasures for your life.

Christian, here you are—you and your Bible. Ignore it or neglect it, and you'll be just like the rest of all those carnal Christians, still

Infants, tossed back and forth by the waves, and blown here and there by every wind of teaching and by the cunning and craftiness of men in their deceitful scheming (Ephesians 4:14).

Instead:

Do your best to present yourself to God as one approved, a workman who does not need to be ashamed and who correctly handles the word of truth (2 Timothy 2:15).

One other thing:

You Can't Keep It to Yourself

The Bible is your message! You as a believer now have the Word of God for the world! That's wonderful! The prophets of the Old Testament said, "Thus saith the Lord," or "This is what the Lord says." You can say the same! In all humility and yet with all the boldness you can tell the world, "This is what the Lord says!"

Christian, you have in your hand the gospel, the good news. This Bible is your life message—and actually, it's your *only* life message. So Paul said to Timothy, "Timothy, give out the truth— in season and out of season, when you feel like it and when you don't."

Do it boldly! The Word of God makes you wiser than the wisest of men who have only the wisdom of this world. Psalm 119:45,46:

I will walk about in freedom, for I have sought out your precepts. I will speak of your statutes before kings and will not be put to shame.

There is nothing, nothing like this wonderful book. All your life, 1 Peter 2:2 says to crave the Word the way new babies crave milk! You'll stay fresh and teachable and eager.

Stay new—through Bible study!

Now go back to Psalm 19:7–11 and make a list of all the Bible *is*—for you. Then make a second list of all the Bible *does*—for you.

His Word will help you "be a new Christian all your life"! Memorize Psalm 119:37.

Questions for Review

1. According to 2 Peter 1:20,21, what does the Bible claim for itself?
2. Can you name the three general sections of the Old Testament and of the New Testament? Which books fit into each section?

3. What does it mean to read the Bible devotionally?
4. The author lists seven things to watch for in reading any passage in the Bible. Name these and tell what each one means.

SIX

Lord, I Want to Stay Continually Cleansed From Sin

For background, first read 1 John 1:1—2:2

"I guess it had to happen."

Sin is your number-one enemy. Being a new Christian—or being a Christian who wants to live in renewal—you've got to know first off how to overcome sin—how to soar, how to fly high.

You've got to know how to get free of the downward drag of being continually discouraged over yourself!

Sin: A Subject We Have to Deal With When Talking About Living in Continual Newness With the Lord

If I wrote this book only on the subject of prayer, or church, or anything else, we'd quickly get unrealistic with each other, you and I; we'd both be hiding behind masks; we'd be uncomfortably aware of the murkiness which seems to lurk here and there under the surfaces of our lives, and which we were trying to avoid!

I know about that murkiness, too. So I don't want to write this book pretending that Ray Ortlund is qualified to write because he's got it all together!

If You're a New Christian

Did you receive the Lord as your Savior recently? A week ago? Six months ago? And at that time you asked Him to forgive all your sins, right? That is, you asked Him to cleanse away everything you'd done wrong from your birth up to that moment. Isn't that true?

But you've committed a lot of sins between that moment and now. What's happening to them?

Maybe they've really disillusioned you by now. Did you expect your life to be totally changed at your conversion, the old problems all gone forever—and since then you've found them still there, big as life? And maybe you're shocked to find that the old drives, the old tendencies to sin haven't gone away after all. And then doubts flood in; the first glow and thrill is gone; nobody's congratulating you or hugging you the way they did . . Maybe you're not even a Christian yet after all!

If You're a Longer-Time Christian

As long as you live on this earth you have to understand sin and know how to handle it in your life. Otherwise you won't live in newness; you'll live in total discouragement!

When I was a boy in church and the preacher would give an invitation to receive Christ, you could depend on it: I'd be his first customer. I was painfully aware of the sins that kept cropping up in my life, and I thought they kept disqualifying me over and over from being a Christian, so I'd have to keep starting again!

Your "Standing" and Your "State"

Get a couple of things straight right away: there's all the difference between crisis and process—or between your standing and your state. Your standing before God is fixed forever; your state changes from moment to moment.

There was the instant of your new birth when God pronounced you His child and credited His perfect righteousness to you (Romans 4:3–5). He didn't do it because your old habits were totally gone; He did it because you said you believed in Him to justify you by His Son's death and resurrection (Romans 4:23–25). That's when you received your standing. That was the crisis.

But then the process began—and it continues relentlessly until the moment when you will see Him as He is, and you'll be perfectly like Him (1 John 3:2).

"Well, how," you're asking, "can God consider me perfectly righteous if I'm still living with the old crud?"

Because God sees you through Christ-colored glasses. He

considers you now in your eternal "standing" before Him. He is looking at the pure sinlessness of His Son, and He stamps in your ledger book that you're like that, too.

Christ's salvation is so powerful that it credits total perfection to your account. No more red ink! All your debts of sin are paid. As a businessman would put it, you're "lookin' good."

Okay, then, can you say "whoopee! I can live it up and sin all I want because God considers me forgiven"?

Romans 6:1 asks that question and answers, in the various translations,

"Of course not!"

"By no means!"

"No, no!"

"What a ghastly thought!"

But it's a process. You're *becoming*, friend. You're not there yet. We sin because we're sinners. The *root* of the problem is sin, singular—that "old nature" still within. The *fruit* of the problem, our sins, plural, keeps cropping up as a result.

I got a staph infection once. If you've never had it, don't bother. It was an infection deep inside me which lasted about seven years. Most of the time I was fine, but because I had that infection lurking inside, I'd never know when a nasty boil was going to break out someplace on my body.

The same is true with me, spiritually. I have a sinful nature inside: that's sin. And sometimes the boils crop out: they're sins. Ask Anne! She knows.

All Christians struggle with the sins in their lives. Samuel Johnson was that wonderful eccentric genius who compiled the first English dictionary. He also faithfully kept a diary, which is a revealing record of his struggle with all the personal resolutions he made every Easter to conquer his sins.

September 18, 1764, he wrote, "Since my resolution formed last Easter, I have made no advancement in knowledge of goodness, nor do I recollect that I have endeavored it. I am dejected but not hopeless."

And then Easter, April 7, 1765: "When I consider how vainly

I hitherto have resolved at this annual commemoration of my Savior's death to regulate my life by his laws, I am almost afraid to renew my resolution. But I will."

Then it was Easter again, in 1779: "Of resolutions I have made so many with so little effect that I am almost weary. But by the help of God, I am not yet hopeless. Good resolutions must be kept and must be made. I am almost seventy years old; I have no time to lose." So we get a picture of the wrestlings of one believer.

But it's never time to roll over and die. You go on! It's always time to dust yourself off and take fresh steps ahead with Christ.

> You may not always live a victorious life, but you always have a victorious Christ!

John White writes in his book *The Fight*:

"Of course you may get wounded in the battle. Of course you may get knocked off your feet, but it is the man or woman who gets back up and fights again that's the warrior.

"What would you think of a soldier who is in the midst of battles, who would sit down and say, 'I'm no good. It's no use trying any more. Nothing seems to work'?

"There's no place for giving up. The warfare is so much bigger than our personal humiliations. Feeling sorry for oneself is totally inappropriate! Over such a soldier I would pour a bucket of icy water; I would drag him to his feet and kick him in the rear end and put his sword in his hand and shout, 'Now fight!' In some circumstances one must be cruel to be kind."

False Claims Some Christians Make

Don't ever claim to be the three things 1 John says you can never be. We find them in 1 John 1:6,8, and 10. They come out of darkness (ignorance), and God in His light speaks out to counter them.

1 John 1:5: "This is the message we have heard from him and declare to you: God is light; in him there is no darkness at all." He is not some doddering old grandfather who can't see and doesn't care.

Our town of Newport Beach employs helicopters that hover over us evenings, checking for burglars or problems. Here we'll be in comfortable semidarkness, and suddenly a little whirlybird is overhead with its powerful beam focusing right on some house in the neighborhood. If there's a robber around in the bushes the light can pin him down and the police move in.

With God, everything is in exposure. Verse 5 says He's light. Verse 7 says He's in the light. Those two things are complimentary, but they're not the same. When God says He's not only light but "in the light," He means that He, too, is in the open, He's exposed, He's transparent, He's knowable!

And that's how you are to be before Him. You're like the

"Nothing personal . . . nothing personal . . . nothing personal. . . ."

burglar in the bushes with God's whirlybird light shining down on you and exposing you totally!

So what can't you claim? You can't claim three things:

1. That you have fellowship with Him if you walk in darkness (v. 6).

2. That you are presently without sin (v. 8).

3. That you have not sinned in the past (v. 10).

Every generation has its own versions of Christianity which make those claims. Beware! Don't join with those who claim to have fellowship with the Lord—but want it on the easiest possible terms. They say everything is great with them when it isn't. They won't look squarely at sin: they soft-pedal it. Avoid those who say it doesn't exist, or who say they've conquered it, or who tamper with it, or who simply ignore it altogether.

God is light! God cannot be fooled!

A man told me once that his wife hadn't sinned in ten years. Imagine! I should have been impressed, but honestly, I was disbelieving.

"You mean to say," I said, "in ten years she hasn't told an untruth, she hasn't gossiped, she's never been unjustly angry, she's never criticized needlessly, she hasn't once lost her temper?"

"Oh, well," he said, "that's just your own definition of sin!"

Now, here's a dangerous thing. If we try to adjust or redefine sin we're doing three things listed here:

1. Verse 6 says we lie.

2. Verse 8 says we deceive ourselves.

3. And verse 10 says we make God out to be a liar, and His Word has no place in our lives. That's heavy duty! Then we are really in trouble. Christian, it is absolutely crucial that you have a correct view of sin.

1 John is saying that true Christianity is healthily realistic. It's saying you can face tough facts of life with courage. It's saying that God is light, and that human attempts to soft-pedal or cover over sin are so much baloney to Him.

So you're the burglar exposed by the helicopter? *Don't stay crouched in the bushes,* says 1 John 1:7! Step right out into the light of God. Make it your lifelong habit, to bravely expose all that you are to all that God is.

1 John 1:7: "If we walk in the light, as he is in the light," two things happen:

1. "We have fellowship with one another"; that is, the two talked about here will stay in fellowship, God and us; and

2. "The blood of Jesus, his Son, purifies us from every sin." The work of initial salvation goes right on smoothly functioning. The same blood of Christ that cleansed you totally at conversion keeps on cleansing you. You stay a new and clean Christian all your life!

How to Tell It Like It Is

Jesus was once teaching in a synagogue, and Luke 6 says a man was there whose hand was all shriveled up. With all the crowds watching, Jesus said to him, "Stretch out your hand."

Now the man could have been embarrassed and just stuck it in his pocket. Instead he simply obeyed. He stretched out his hand, and when he acknowledged his problem Jesus healed it!

That's what Proverbs 28:13 is saying: "He who conceals [covers] his sins does not prosper, but whoever confesses and renounces them finds mercy."

Here's a person who's got sin in his life. He tries to cover it over. God comes along and He says, "Wait a minute, I want you to look at that," and He uncovers it.

"No, I don't want to see it," the fellow says, and he covers it over again. We have a tug-of-war going on here, and God is going to win!

You see, what you try to cover, at the Judgment Day God will uncover. But when you confess—uncover your sin—God will cover it; He will show mercy. That's what the word *atonement* means: a covering for our sins. Confess the whole mess; admit it totally, and the blood of Jesus will continually be God's merciful atonement for you.

The Swiss psychologist Carl Jung said, "Because we cannot face the greater sin, we often confess some lesser sin all the more earnestly. But there is no real relief because there is no real confession."

God can't stand baloney! He is light! Be real with Him, Christian!

Now in recent years the need for cleansing has seemed so desperate, there have been weird group experiments in confession. I really don't think those are the solution God had in mind! But *somewhere*, some way—just to God, to the one offended, to your small group, perhaps—you need to confess your sins. Christians who never confess anything get all bottled up.

The word *confess* is made up of two Greek words, *homo*, which means "alike," and *lego*, "to say." *Confess* in Greek is *homolego*, to say the same thing that the Spirit of God is saying to you.

God says, "What you just said was wrong." You can't explain it but there's that sense of conviction inside of you: "Uh oh, that was wrong." And when you say quickly, "Lord, I was wrong," you're saying back to God what He just said to you: "You're wrong."

Confession is not regret or remorse or tears. To confess is simply to agree. It doesn't keep you emotionally unstrung; it just keeps you cleansed and in fellowship with Him.

Your foot's heavy on the gas pedal. God says, "You shouldn't be speeding." If you say, "Well, Lord, everybody's doing it," you're going to get into deeper trouble. If you say, "I shouldn't be speeding," you're agreeing with God, you're in fellowship, you're confessing.

Then slow down!

You know, as you walk with God in the light, you'll find that you confess more and more while you seem to sin a bit less and less. But when you confess less and less, you're going to sin more and more.

Continually Walk in the Light—in Honesty With God

Then there's fellowship with Him; you're not hiding anything. You're saying, "Lord, You know the whole bag." And He's saying, "I know. But the blood of Jesus, My Son, is cleansing you."

Remember it's the blood of Jesus, not your confession, that cleanses. It isn't even your humility or your tears. It's your Savior! It's His work on the cross, His atoning sacrifice which is powerful to purify you from every sin.

You experience, then, constant fellowship with God. It's a great thing to be open and humble and continually fresh in your relationship with God almighty!

Wonderful verse 9: "If we confess our sins, he is faithful and just and will forgive us our sins and purify us from all unrighteousness."

He's both faithful and just when He forgives us.

Dennis the Menace was saying his evening prayers, kneeling beside his bed.

"Why are you whispering?" his mother asked. "I can't hear you."

"Because," said Dennis, "I know God will forgive me, but I'm not so sure about you!"

God will! He does! He is faithful; you can count on His being continually loving and forgiving. He doesn't change.

And He's just when He purifies us. He doesn't have to say, "Okay, we'll forget it. But don't do it again." He can cleanse us with all good conscience because He made provision for it through the sacrifice of His Son.

And the promise is so lavish! He'll purify you "from all unrighteousness"! When you confess the sins you know, He'll forgive all the rest you *don't* know as well!

In the Old Testament there were sacrifices for the sins of ignorance. People really needed those sacrifices, too, because nobody knows how much he sins; none of us has any idea. So God even provided sacrifices for the sins that *He* knew about, but they were unaware of.

That's what confession continually does for you. 1 John 1:9 says that when you confess what you know, He forgives those plus all the rest! He's fabulous!

Your Salvation Provides for Total Protection

"My dear children," writes John to all of us today, "I write this to you so that you will not sin. But if anybody does sin, we have one who speaks to the Father in our defense—Jesus Christ, the Righteous One. He is the atoning sacrifice for our sins, and not only for ours but also for the sins of the whole world" (1 John 2:1,2).

Wonderful Jesus! He's double protection: He's both your lawyer and your sacrifice. When you confess, He speaks to the Father on your behalf, as your older Brother to protect the honor of the family of God.

And He's also your "sin offering," reminding a pure, holy God that your sins were thoroughly paid for. Christ in every way has satisfied the requirements of God for righteousness.

And He died for the whole world. What does that mean?

Well, salvation is offered to everybody. It's totally sufficient for the whole world. But it's only efficient for those who accept it by faith. God holds out His wonderful present—but those who don't reach out their hand and take it still haven't got it.

A wonderful truth: If God's forgiveness is great enough to be offered to everybody in the world, He's not going to run out of it before He gets through with you.

Don't ever say, "My sin is so awful, I don't know if God will forgive me." He has tons and heaps and gobs of forgiveness for the whole world. If Jesus told His disciples to forgive each other seventy times seven, He will forgive you seventy times seven plus, plus—! You can depend on it.

When our son Ray, Jr., was a student at Wheaton College, I was visiting him, and I noticed a paper on his desk. I'm not the snoopy type, but I couldn't help noticing that he struggles as his dad does. On the paper Bud had written, "I'm so full of myself, I'm so frustrated, I'm so defeated, I'm so discouraged, I'm so sad." Then he'd written a great big "BUT," and from there on the words got bigger and bigger: "Christ is sufficient! Christ is victorious! Christ is sovereign! Christ is capable! Christ is loving! And I'm forgiven—so press on!!"

Hey, do you like this chapter? You should. It's good news. I'm saying that 1 John 1 says to you,

"Hang tough.
"Don't run.
"Face the facts.
"Admit the truth.
"Rejoice in God's forgiveness, and,
"Walk in the light!"

Questions for Review

1. What's the difference between your "standing" as a Christian, and your "state"?
2. Concerning sin, what are three things the Christian cannot say, according to 1 John?
3. Why is it futile for us to try to hide our sins from God?
4. What does it mean to confess our sins? And what does God promise to do if we confess? To whom should we confess, and when?

SEVEN

Lord, I Want to Stay Liberated

For background, first read Romans 7:1—8:4

"Toad baked some cookies. 'These cookies smell very good,' said Toad. He ate one. 'And they taste even better,' he said. Toad ran to Frog's house. 'Frog, Frog,' cried Toad, 'taste these cookies that I have made.'

"Frog ate one of the cookies. 'These are the best cookies I have ever eaten!' said Frog.

"Frog and Toad ate many cookies, one after another. 'You know, Toad,' said Frog, with his mouth full, 'I think we should stop eating. We will soon be sick.'

" 'You are right,' said Toad. 'Let us eat one last cookie, and then we will stop.' Frog and Toad ate one last cookie. There were many cookies left in the bowl.

" 'Frog,' said Toad, 'let us eat one very last cookie, and then we will stop.' Frog and Toad ate one very last cookie.

" 'We must stop eating!' cried Toad as he ate another.

" 'Yes,' said Frog, reaching for a cookie, 'we need will power.'

" 'What is will power?' asked Toad.

" 'Will power is trying hard not to do something that you really want to do,' said Frog.

" 'You mean like trying hard not to eat all these cookies?' asked Toad.

" 'Right,' said Frog.

"Frog put the cookies in a box. 'There,' he said. 'Now we will not eat any more cookies.'

" 'But we can open the box,' said Toad.

" 'That is true,' said Frog.

"Frog tied some string around the box. 'There,' he said. 'Now we will not eat any more cookies.'

" 'But we can cut the string and open the box,' said Toad

" 'That is true,' said Frog.

"Frog got a ladder. He put the box up on a high shelf. 'There,' said Frog. 'Now we will not eat any more cookies.'

" 'But we can climb the ladder and take the box down from the shelf and cut the string and open the box,' said Toad.

" 'That is true,' said Frog.

"Frog climbed the ladder and took the box down from the shelf. He cut the string and opened the box.

"Frog took the box outside. He shouted in a loud voice, 'Hey, birds, here are cookies!' Birds came from everywhere. They picked up all the cookies in their beaks and flew away.

" 'Now we have no more cookies to eat,' said Toad sadly. 'Not even one.'

" 'Yes,' said Frog, 'but we have lots and lots of will power.'

" 'You may keep it all, Frog,' said Toad. 'I am going home now to bake a cake.' "[6]

Toad is obviously not liberated. He's chained to his love of

cookies, as you are chained to your love of _____
_____. (You can fill in the blank.)

We're all chained to something—to lots of things! And whether you're a new Christian or an older one seeking to start fresh, it may scare you to think of that long Christian life stretching out there ahead of you. You may wonder whether you can really break loose of the old habits and loves and get liberated enough to really achieve it.

Well, Romans chapter 7 doesn't help you any. It says:

The Christian life isn't hard; it's impossible.

Face it right away: you can't live the Christian life. I can't live it. Only Jesus ever could or did. If you're trying to in your own strength, you're already worried and uptight.

Sometimes people say, "Well, I believe that if a person believes in Christ and does the best he can, he'll be all right." That may sound good, but it doesn't work. Because no one ever does the best he can.

Do you?

When did you do the best you could? Did you for five minutes? For five hours?

So Romans 3:23 says, "All have sinned and fall short of the glory of God." You just can't get up there to God's glory by your own efforts.

People try to urge you on, like a cheering section: "Witness! Read your Bible! Pray every day! Memorize verses! Give a lot! Forgive everybody! Smile! Cry!"

But after a while you'll be saying, "I just can't do it all. Maybe some people are naturally religious. It's just not my thing."

THE FAR SIDE   By GARY LARSON

Reprinted by permission of Chronicle Features, San Francisco

So Romans 7 tells us about three laws:

1. THE LAW OF PERFECT RIGHTEOUSNESS, which is high, holy, wonderful—and unattainable;

2. THE LAW OF SIN, which keeps you from obeying it; and

3. THE LAW OF THE SPIRIT, which sets you free from it.

**One: The Law of Perfect Righteousness
(Romans 7:1–14)**

Let's say this LAW OF PERFECT RIGHTEOUSNESS is a husband. He's impeccable—in his grooming, his habits, everything. He is always correct, and he expects his wife to be too. He's pretty dominating, but actually, everything he asks of her is absolutely right. So every morning he outlines her schedule for the day, and every moment is full of good things. When he leaves for work there's his checklist, and it must all be done and done on time.

But here's this wife: she's the second Law. She's slow, forgetful, easygoing. She's a bit sloppy with her housework. She has a built-in drag. She tries hard, but not for very long!

Well, when the husband comes home the place is a wreck. He takes out the list and he says, "8:00 to 8:30, you were supposed to do the breakfast dishes. Did you?" "No."

"8:30 to 9:00 you were to make the beds and straighten and dust. Did you get those things done?"

And she says, "No. Boo-hoo-hoo! I was tired, and I didn't feel well, and I couldn't do anything today."

Now you see, she's under condemnation.

And she'd like to sing that old song:

> Why don't we get along?
> Everything I do is wrong;
> Tell me, what's the reason
> I'm not pleasin' you?

But this fellow never lifts a finger to help her; he just keeps ruthlessly checking off the list.

Of course *the things he asks of her are absolutely right.* But let's face it: the marriage is not a success. In fact they are hopelessly incompatible.

In the same way you, as an ordinary human being, just can't perfectly attain God's standard of righteousness. Even as a Christian you just can't please "the Law."

Well, that night she lies in bed thinking, *How can I get out of this marriage? Maybe on the way to work in the morning he'll get killed.* . . . *Oh, I shouldn't think that!*

This is the situation Romans 7:2,3 is speaking of:

> By law a married woman is bound to her husband as long as he is alive, but if her husband dies, she is released from the law of marriage.
>
> So then, if she marries another man while her husband is still alive, she is called an adulteress.
>
> But if her husband dies, she is released from that law and is not an adulteress, even though she marries another man.

But the point is, he's the Law, and God says, "Heaven and earth will pass away, but my words [the Law] will never pass away." This marriage is not going to be dissolved by his death.

So, is the poor wife stuck? And are you stuck with THE LAW OF PERFECT RIGHTEOUSNESS, that you can't possibly please and fulfill?

Living with the Law makes an impossible marriage. The Old Testament Israelites discovered that. They couldn't measure up, and neither can you.

Why? Because of—

Two: The Law of Sin, Which Keeps You From Obeying the Law of Righteousness (Romans 7:15–25)

Even the great Apostle Paul struggled with the same thing:

> So I find this law at work: When I want to do good, evil is right there with me. For in my inner being I delight in God's law; but I see another law at work in the members of my body, waging war against the law of my mind and making me a prisoner of the law of sin at work within my members. What a wretched man I am! . . .

There is a power within you that's an inbuilt resister to the will of God. Its name is THE LAW OF SIN.

A Christian I know tells what his life was like "B.C." Driving home from work each day the temptation was to stop at a certain bar, but he knew he'd stay too long and his family would get mad over his drinking too much.

So to keep from going in, as soon as he got into his car he'd pull off his shoes and socks, because you don't ever go into a bar without shoes and socks on. Then he'd pull off his tie, and he'd pull off his shirt, and he'd be saying to himself, *Now I can't go into the bar.*

But as he drove down the Pasadena Freeway from Los Angeles, he'd get about to Avenue 64 and he'd be pulling at his socks; and as he kept driving he'd be toeing his way into his shoes. On would go his shirt, and when he got to the bar he'd go in.

Why? "What I hate I do" (verse 15). It's a picture of you and me.

A preacher was eloquently quoting Rudyard Kipling's poem "If." With great drama he read,

If you can fill the unforgiving minutes
With sixty seconds' worth of distance run—

and a voice from the back called out despairingly, "But what if you can't?"

There is the absolute necessity of despair. When Paul in Romans 7:24 cried out, "What a wretched man I am! Who will rescue me from this body of death?"—I think all heaven began to say, "Well, praise the Lord! Maybe Paul's about to get the answer!"

That's just the point where God can help you. As long as you think you can live the Christian life all by yourself, you'll fall on your face over and over. You must come to realize *you can't do it*—and the sooner, the better.

You see, just as you could not save yourself, you cannot pull

Reprinted by permission of Tribune Company Syndicate, Inc.

yourself up by your own bootstraps. To be saved you need the love and grace of Jesus Christ with all that He did at Calvary to forgive your sins and to be to you saving grace. You could not do that by human willpower. So you cannot live the Christian life by human willpower. The whole thing from beginning to end is on the basis of the work and worth of Jesus Christ.

Your Christian life was begun by grace (God's loving favor). It was all God's doing. And *it must continue by grace.*

I know Christians say this is true—maybe you do—but honestly, has it taken that eighteen-inch trip yet—out of your head and into your heart?

The Holy Spirit started it all; you're not a Christian by accident or by your own design. He put you in places to expose you to His Word, and He aroused you to believe it. *God loved you to Himself.*

And that's the way it continues to happen: *God continues loving you to Himself.* Your life is not so different from your birth.

Too many think of conversion as a relationship and the Christian life as a religion (a lifestyle of doing good works). No, no! Christianity must be a relationship from start to finish.

A friend of mine says that every Christian must experience "the second crash." The first "crash" came when you saw you were spiritually bankrupt, a sinner with no righteousness to present to God on your own. But you found that "Jesus paid it all," and you trusted in Him alone to save you.

The "second crash" comes when you see you can't even live the Christian life on your own. You're constantly in debt to Him. And the only thing to help you is trusting Jesus Christ to live His righteousness in you, and letting your life continue to be all of Him.

Look again at the parable of the bad marriage (Romans 7). We discovered that the Law will never pass away, so the marriage couldn't be dissolved by his death.

Well, if he couldn't die then what's the way out? *She must die.*

But wouldn't that ruin everything? No, it's the only way to save the situation.

Look at verses 4 and 6:

> So, my brothers, you also died to the law through the body of Christ, that you might belong to another, to him who was raised from the dead....
>
> Now, by dying to what once bound us, we have been released from the law so that we serve in the new way of the Spirit, and not in the old way of the written code.

Three: The Law of the Spirit, Which Sets You Free From the Old Law (Romans 7:25—8:11)

As a new Christian, despair over yourself is your greatest need. Welcome it! Romans 7 calls it the death of self.

When you die, you're no longer answerable to that meticulous, impossible husband, the Law. He can be as "wonderful" as ever, but he just doesn't have any hold over you! You're dead. You're free.

And now—what a miracle!—verse 4 says that your identification with Christ means that as He was resurrected, you're resurrected—to enjoy a new husband, even the same gloriously risen Christ!

Here He is, your wonderful new Husband, who stands beside you in your weakness and helps you, cares for you, works for you, encourages you, surrounds you, loves you, and is kind to you!

The identification is so complete, you're even given His perfect righteousness, which the Law was powerless to give you! And the new LAW OF THE SPIRIT in your life will lift and restore and renew you, as often as you call upon it.

I was jogging on the beach a week or two ago and I ran across the carcass of a dead sea gull. I love to watch the gulls soar as they use the currents of the air; they're beautiful.

But if I'd taken that dead carcass and thrown it into the air and said, "Fly, gull!" it would have fallen by the power of gravity with a thud at my feet. There was no life there.

The same power of gravity is at work on the gull that's flying, but there's life inside. There's the power of life within.

Christian, God has put within you THE LAW OF THE SPIRIT, a mighty, overcoming power, to cause you to soar for God.

All your life you'll be aware of THE LAW OF SIN, the drag, the downward pull; but you have a greater power within you. Sin is great, but the power of Christ is greater. Grace is much more abundant! It's superabundant!

> If Christ is in you, your body is dead because of sin, yet your spirit is alive because of righteousness. And if the Spirit of him who raised Jesus from the dead is living in you, he who raised Christ from the dead will also give life to your mortal bodies through his Spirit, who lives in you (Romans 8:10,11).

You may be sometimes defeated momentarily; so am I. "What I want to do I do not do, but what I hate I do" (Romans 7:15). It's the story of my life every day—unless I remember that I have one recourse, and that's to live by THE LAW OF THE SPIRIT— that is, by the strength of and in the power of the One who dwells within me.

A new Christian came to see me recently—that is, an almost new Christian. And he'd just arrived at his first danger point, his first temptation to sag.

He said, "I want to tell you what's happened to me. When I came to Christ I was all alone at home. There, all by myself, the Lord met me and helped me understand that He had died on the cross to take my place in punishment for my sin. His light of understanding flooded my heart. I received His gift of forgiveness.

"It was awesome! Without anyone suggesting it, I began to read my Bible. And I began to tell others what had happened to me. And I loved to pray."

He went on, "Then I met a teacher who pointed his finger at me and said, 'If you want to please the Lord you *must* witness; you *must* pray; you *must* read your Bible.'

"That's just what I'd been doing," he said, "but now he made me feel it was an obligation; it was a duty I had to perform in order to please God.

"All was fine—until I didn't do it. There came a day when I didn't read my Bible, I didn't pray, and I didn't witness. Then I felt I was a failure, I thought God must be angry with me, and I felt under a big burden of guilt."

But he said, "I think I found the answer. I was reading Romans 7, and I found out that in myself I really can't please the Lord anyway. Laws to do this and that just tie me up in hopelessness.

"But God hasn't given me laws to live by; He's given me Jesus Christ! I can live in the strength of Christ; I don't have to live in my own strength. He's the one who pleases God, so it has to be not my doing, but His doing!"

Well, I thought, *he's really got it! He's nailed down one of the key truths to Christian success. He's going to go a long way; he'll stay liberated!*

Questions for Review

1. What's wrong with the notion: "I'll believe in Christ and do the best that I can"? Why isn't that good enough?

2. What are the three laws Romans 7 tells us about?
3. Why should the Christian *welcome* the knowledge that he can never live the Christian life in his own strength?
4. What are areas in your own life where you might be tempted to "do it all by yourself"?

"Be perfect," God says to you in Matthew 5:48.

"Be *what*?" you say. "I'm a new Christian, I'm immature, and I don't know much. 'Be perfect'? No chance!"

Well, you look at a tight baby rosebud sometime, and you say, "Isn't that bud just perfect?"

If you see it a while later, half open, you say, "Look at that perfect rose!"

Days later you may catch it at its fullest maturity, and you say, "Oh, that rose is absolutely perfect!"

So you can be perfect at every stage of your Christian development. "Perfect" means wanting to be all that God wants you to be, at any given moment.

Christian, "be perfect." From right now on.

EIGHT

Lord, I Need Meaningful Relationships With Others

For background, first read Ephesians 4:1–6

Humpty Dumpty:
"I was pushed."

It's a hostile world out there. Non-Christians tend to excuse themselves and accuse everybody else. It's snarl-shove-and-hit to survive.

If you're a new Christian, you've come into something wonderfully different! You came through the door into Christ single file, but from that moment on, in Him you have family, and you have lavish resources for love and support.

103

Understand these resources and how to take advantage of them. Then all your life your relationship with Christ and with other Christians can just continually sweeten and deepen and grow. Not that there won't be sticky times, but you've also got great things going for you.

We've already said that you need to readjust your life to three all-important commitments:

One, to the Lord Jesus Christ Himself;

Two, to your fellow believers in Christ; and

Three, to your work for Christ in this world.[7]

God wants to give your life order and system and balance. A biblical lifestyle isn't complicated! It's not just for ministers and spiritual "heavies"! Reshape your life to Christ, to the body of Christ, and to the world for whom Christ died. One, two, three.

Priority One must be the top priority! First before anything you must love and worship God. So must I.

And second, we must love the church universal, all fellow believers everywhere. God does—and our hearts must follow His heart.

What Does "The Church" Mean?

There are churches within the church. The church universal is made up of all believers in Christ of all time: the "body of Christ" (pictured here as the large church). The members of a local, organized church may be totally within the true church universal; or they may be partly in and partly out, with some only giving lip service to Christ; or they may be totally outside, with not one actually born again.

The Book of Ephesians tells you fabulous things about the church. For instance:

> And God placed all things under [Christ's] feet and appointed him to be head over everything for the church, which is his body, the fullness of him who fills everything in every way (Ephesians 1:22,23).

The church, the true family of God, believers in Christ, is called a *body*. And this body is to have Christ as its priority. He is the Head. He is the Top. He is Priority Number One to every one of us. He is the intellect. He is in control.

And we are His body. The true church is not an organization—

It's not a building—

It's not a denomination.

The church is pictured in the Bible as a living organism. And each individual Christian has become a part of it—throbbing with life! Says one commentator, "That is the boldest, the most magnificent image or figure used in the Bible. . . . Beyond that nothing higher can be pictured or imagined."

Christ makes us a living part of Himself! Think of a great image, so tall the head is up in the clouds, out of sight. Well, He calls Himself the Head, invisible from earth; and we are His body, visible and to be reckoned with by all who live on earth.

And yet we are truly one with Him, truly connected with our unseen Head. A head needs a body as much as a body needs a head. Verse 23 says we are His fullness; we fulfill Him! He has an inner craving for you and me, a desire for His people so great that He makes us a living part of Himself—that part of Him which expresses Him, His body. How exciting! How fabulous!

It's a sacred relationship, then, that we have, not only with Him but with each other. We are dependent on each other as parts of the body are, and we have a sacred priority to each other, to nourish and help each other.

Five Ways to Love the Church

One: Love the Church by Uniting in Membership

Unity: God says we have it—but we're to express it.

How do you reconcile these two statements, side by side in Ephesians 4:3–6?

Make every effort to keep the unity of the Spirit through the bond of peace.	There is one body and one Spirit—just as you were called to one hope when you were called—one Lord, one faith, one baptism; one God and Father of all, who is over all and through all and in all.

Nobody ever figured out the mind of God (Romans 11:33–36). Many times in the New Testament He says "so-and-so is true. Now make it true in your life!" Look for these as you read.

Here He says to the church, "You *are* unified. Now *be* unified."

How are you to express your unity, your togetherness? For one thing, by joining a local group of believers. Make sure you're a member. It's a form of deep commitment—of the Second Priority. Ask God to show you which church: hopefully, if you have a choice, where Christ is exalted and where His Word is taught and where the people love each other. It won't be perfect; do the best you can and don't be totally picky.

But join some local Christian church. A local church is a visible expression of the true church universal, and you need to give your heart to a group of people who name His Name. It may not be 100 percent genuine as is the ages-wide mystical Body—but how do you get hold of the true church at all except through a local congregation?

And then praise it, love it, protect it, defend it, identify with it, and serve in it.

Two: Love the Church by Being Baptized and by Taking Communion

What form of baptism? How often Communion? Humbly submit to whatever your church fathers recommend. The church has so often been divided over kinds of baptism and Communion! How it must grieve the Spirit of God, when the thing He pleads for is unity!

Don't be fussy. In a tense world, when believers are apt to catch the world's disease and bicker with each other, one of your greatest contributions can be prayerful, optimistic, happy, loving support.

Three: Love the Church by Committing Yourself

When you identify with a local body, with real flesh and blood people, you're in for a ride. Maybe you're in for such a jolt you'll get whiplash!

Somebody said:

> To live above with saints we love,
> That will be grace and glory.
> To live below with saints we know—
> Well, that's another story!

That's why Ephesians 4:3 says, "Make every effort." Have the attitude of looking them in the eye and saying, in effect, "There is nothing you could do, nothing you could tell me, that would make me love you any less than I do right now."

> Be imitators of God, therefore, as dearly loved children and live a life of love, just as Christ loved us and gave

"At the count of three, I want everyone to face the person next to him and get rid of your hostilities and be happy human beings."

© 1980. Reprinted by permission of *Leadership* and Joseph Farris.

himself up for us as a fragrant offering and sacrifice to God (Ephesians 5:1,2).

An offering costs. A sacrifice may involve pain. But when we disregard our natural inclinations and love each other *"as Christ loved us"*—sins, scars, mars, and all—our love for our fellow Christians becomes a fragrance, a sweet smelling perfume, to the Lord.

Romans 15:7 says to "accept one another . . . just as Christ accepted you, in order to bring praise to God." The loving church has a fragrance about it—and so does the loving church member. Christian, vow to be one of those! Vow to love continually not only the Lord but His body!

When problems come (as they will) don't get cynical. Remember, nobody's perfect yet—but if they're genuine Christians then one day they will be. Rejoice in their future condition if not in their present.[8]

Four: Love the Church by Offering It Your Gifts

It was [Christ] who gave some to be apostles, some to be prophets, some to be evangelists, and some to be pastors

"I think we'd better buy smaller letters and spell the word out."

© *Leadership* magazine. Artist Larry Thomas. Used by permission.

and teachers, to prepare God's people for works of service, so that the body of Christ may be built up until we all reach unity in the faith and in the knowledge of the Son of God and become mature, attaining to the whole measure of the fullness of Christ (Ephesians 4:11–13).

Congregations aren't to be just docile flocks of sheep that file into church on a Sunday morning, listen to something, and file out again.

A rector's family in the Church of England wrote this little poem, which is a takeoff on another poem you may remember:

> The pastor is late,
>   He's forgotten the date,
> So what can the faithful do now,
>   Poor things?
> They'll sit in a pew
>   With nothing to do,
> And sing a selection of hymns,
>   Poor things!

Well, what's Priority Two all about? We Christians have to fit all our "parts" together. We're responsible members, aggressive participants. The church isn't the pastor's show. The church must be the whole body—the eyes, ears, hands, feet. . . . It's functioning, serving each other, loving each other. It's taking care of each other's children in Sunday school. It's fitting in where God has given you a gift—in the choir, or as ushers. It's teaching. It's caring. It's being aunts and uncles to one another's children. It's being all this in the family of God, and it includes both single people and married people. We're all in this together. It's adapting ourselves to the family of God.[9]

How can you discover what your particular gifts are? Don't worry about it. Lately I think there's been too much self-analyzing and self-occupation over this. Just have the attitude of "What can I do to help?"—and as you begin to serve, the things you do best and most happily will emerge.

"Last year we 'reached the world.' This year we're 'sharing and caring.' "

When we first went to Lake Avenue Congregational Church in Pasadena, Anne was asked to cook the vegetables for a congregational dinner. When three hundred people had to wait twenty minutes for the beans to boil and cook, they never asked her to do that again. They'd discovered what one of her gifts was *not*! Anne is really great but a cook she ain't!

Eventually she got to teach a lot of Bible classes.

Five: Love the Church by Being in a Small Group

Every local church suffers from too many "hi" Christians. I don't mean liturgically "high"; I mean they just give you "Hi!"—"Hi, how are you?"—"Oh, hi!"—and that's all you get. Maybe they have a cup of coffee with you and talk about a football game or something. But if they never cry with anyone, if they never help lift the one who's fallen into sin, if they never share where they hurt—they are living very superficial lives.

I know Christians who never tell anyone when they have

problems. (But what's new about having problems?) So they never get anywhere with each other in true friendships. It seems almost vulgar to know Jesus Christ and never really go to the throne in deep concern for each other, or go to the Word together to dig out the truths of God.

When Jesus gave us the new commandment to "love one another" (John 13:34,35), He didn't mean as "hi Christians." He pointed to a deeper way; and how do we structure it?

The way, the structure, is a small group of four to eight Christians that you gather with week by week, to love God and love each other together. I know of no adequate substitute for this, no second choice.

The English preacher John Stott says of small groups, "They are indispensable for Christian growth and maturity." I don't believe you will ever go on to the extent God would have you, as long as you resist being in a small group. You need to be in the Word with another brother and sister at close range. This is what the early church did; it's part of what it is to be a Christian.

What should happen in a small group?

First, worship God together. Just look up to God together in prayer or through a hymn, and tell Him you love Him.

Second, feed on the Word of God together. Take turns leading, or ask an older Christian to disciple you and lead you. But don't let it be just a Bible study. It's too easy to "discuss," impersonally.

Third, share your joys and burdens in your group. Let these few close ones know where you are spiritually, and how you'd like help.

Fourth, pray for each other. And know where those brothers or sisters are going to be the next day, during the next week— and keep praying.

You ought also to eat together. I like that, don't you? The Bible is realistic. Acts 2, giving the lifestyle of the early church, says, "They devoted themselves to the apostles' teaching"—that's the Bible, the New Testament; "to fellowship"—that's really sharing your heart; "to the breaking of bread"—something happens when we eat together; "and to prayer."

That's beautiful. That's what you do in a small group. I encourage you to find your way to some other Christians for close support.

Does the thought of it spook you out? Sometimes believers have to get desperate before they'll try it. I can tell you from my own experience how important this has become.

I'd been pastor of Lake Avenue Church for about nine years, and I was at a crisis. Some church leaders were in a committee with me and I told them, "I really have to have people who are going to stand with me in the ministry, shoulder to shoulder; who are going to love me as a person and support me and correct me and help me and lift me."

I said, "I'd like you eight men to commit two hours a week for us to meet together to do four things: to worship the Lord, to share in the Scriptures, to share our life situations, and to pray for each other. In the midst of it all there'll be accountability to one another, to help us grow and improve."

So I asked them for two hours a week. At first there wasn't a lot of response, but finally one said, "Pastor Ray, I'm really busy, and that's a big hunk of time for every single week."

Another said, "I love you, Pastor, but—I'm busy, too."

Brother! I began to think. *This is never going to work.*

Still the talk meandered along . . .

Finally my dear friend Ted spoke up, and with his chin quivering, he said, "Fellows, this is not a discussion time; this is an altar call."

And he went around the circle and asked them one by one. Each guy said yes.

For about a year we met weekly and shared our hearts together. None of us will ever be the same. Since that time God has led me into the lives of about two hundred men, in groups of six to eight. And it has changed my heart and life.

If you want specific "how to's" to help you get started, let me recommend Anne's book *Discipling One Another*. It comes out of all our experiences separately and together, and the experiences of hundreds of small groups around the world that we've observed and encouraged.

If You're Ever Afraid You'll Run Out of Love

You want to love the church—but it might get hot in there.

You'd like to experience a small group—but what if they turn out to be lemons? Well, first let me get tough. Jesus said, "A new commandment I give to you, that you love one another" (John 13:34). It's not an option. It's not an elective.

It's something God tells you you must do—and then He gives you all the resources to do it.

What God demands of you, He will supply to you. Here's a wonderful verse; read it carefully:

> God has poured out his love into our hearts by the Holy Spirit, whom he has given us (Romans 5:5).

You say you just "can't love so-and-so"? If you're a Christian, then

> God has already given to you
> All the love you will ever need,
> For all the people you will ever meet,
> In all the situations you'll ever face.

There's not one Christian without the Holy Spirit. "If anyone does not have the Spirit of Christ, he does not belong to Christ," says Romans 8:9.

So when you received Jesus, you received the Holy Spirit; and from the time you received Him He has kept pouring into your life an inexhaustible supply of the love of God. No one will ever run out of that love. You don't have to worry that your supply will be depleted. "The fruit of the Spirit is love."

Just draw on it and draw on it. Don't suppress it but express it! God has given you an artesian well of love. Don't try to cap it; let it flow.

When your old nature rises up in you with its inhibitions or its hostilities, take it right to the cross. Crucify it daily, and build into your life that for which you already have every resource: those kinds of contacts and activities that allow for the expression of Christ's love within you toward His body.

There's a bumper sticker that says, "Have you hugged your kid today?" That's where it all begins—at home. Draw on the Holy Spirit to make your love within your family circle grow and deepen more and more, whether they know Jesus yet or not!

Then let it spread to your church, and to all your other brothers and sisters in the Lord. Help God's family circle to be a loving place of fellowship!

And out of the larger body of Christ, let a small group particularly be the laboratory where your love is given and received at close range. Plenty of Christians are hurting these days.

Christian relationships: they're so crucial to your nourishment and growth!

The members of the body all need you.

And you need all of them!

Questions for Review

1. What is the church? Who is its Head and who are its members?
2. Discuss the five ways you can prove your love for Christ's body, the church.
3. What is the value of being a part of a small group of committed Christians? What things should such a group seek to do together?

NINE

Lord, Show Me How to Reproduce Myself

For background, first read John 1:35–51

Do you remember the television show "Laugh In"? For a full hour you got whizz-bang antics, joke piling upon joke, one guffaw after another, action upon action.

But remember how it ended? With the applause of just one person. And then the claps getting sparser and sparser. Then one final clap. And the show was over.

The New Testament, on the other hand, begins with John the Baptist's solitary clap for Jesus. Then it builds and builds, with more and more joining in through the Gospels and the Book of Acts, until in Revelation numberless multitudes are around the throne of heaven, giving themselves in a tumult of hallelujahs and praise. Millions upon millions applauding the Lord Jesus!

Christian, in your office or neighborhood or whatever, God is asking you to be one clap for Jesus Christ.

But don't think that your lonely clap will be the end. Christ doesn't program failure. He said, 'I will build my church, and the gates of Hades will not overcome it" (Matthew 16:18). Not everyone will join in the clapping, but multitudes will.

Models for Witnessing: John and Andrew

So there's John the Baptist being solitary applause for Christ. He said "in the words of Isaiah the prophet, 'I am the voice of one calling in the desert, "Make straight the way for the Lord" ' " (John 1:23). And he was one person who became many. Said the prophet Isaiah, "The least of you will become a thousand" (Isaiah 60:22).

Sure enough, others began to applaud the One John was applauding. Followers of John began to want to follow Jesus:

> Andrew, Simon Peter's brother, was one of the two who heard what John had said and who had followed Jesus. The first thing Andrew did was to find his brother Simon and tell him, "We have found the Messiah" (that is, the Christ) (John 1:40,41).

So John the Baptist reached people to bring them to Jesus Christ, who in turn brought people to Jesus Christ. That's the way God does it. It's His program—but it's through people. And Andrew was a little-known person but he brought somebody really important to know the Lord—his brother Simon Peter.

Who are the people around you who need to come to know Jesus? The most natural contacts are our "Simon Peters," our relatives.

Last week I was leading an evangelistic Bible study, and I said at the end, "For the sake of the ones here who haven't received Christ yet, I'd like for some of you to tell how you came to know Him."

Immediately a lovely lady said, "It was through my teenage son. When I saw how he became a different person, I knew I wanted that in my life too."

It made me think about family contacts. Jim and Peggy, a couple along with Anne and me, had founded that Bible study a few years before, and Peggy's brother was the first one in the group to trust the Lord.

When I was growing up it was my two big brothers, living all-out for Christ before me, who influenced me to want to do the same.

Andrew found his brother Peter.

Another Model for Witnessing: Christ Himself

"The next day Jesus decided to leave for Galilee. Finding Philip, he said to him, 'Follow me' " (John 1:43).

Jesus was a relentless Shepherd after lost sheep. And He asked for a large commitment. He said to a man in the middle of his busy life, "Philip, leave everything and follow Me. Come after Me. Be with Me."

And, interestingly, following Jesus became contagious. What resulted when Philip followed Jesus? Nathanael trotted along (John 1:45–49), and soon others.

John 3 finds Jesus in evening conversation with Nicodemus, a Big Shot. He was a Pharisee and a member of the Sanhedrin (the Jewish supreme court).

To him Jesus talked with simple earnestness about the necessity for a new birth: "I tell you the truth, unless a man is born again, he cannot see the kingdom of God" (3:3).

He talked philosophically: "Flesh gives birth to flesh, but the Spirit gives birth to spirit . . ." (3:6).

He talked to him (as He always did when witnessing) personally: "You are Israel's teacher, and do you not understand these things?" (3:10).

He gave him His time, His patience, His courtesy—and Nicodemus became a believer. We know that because later he defended Jesus to the rest of the court (John 7:50,51), and at the end he gave Jesus' body a proper burial (John 19:38–42).

A supreme court justice—and then a Bad Woman.

He found her at a Samaritan well (John 4) and after relaxing over a drink of water, he moved in for a clear "yes" of faith and commitment.

His witnessing on this occasion was very different from when He spoke to Nicodemus. He got right to her lifestyle: "The fact is, you have had five husbands, and the man you now have is not your husband" (4:18).

Sounds too frontal? You may sometimes be led this way of the Spirit! Soon she was witnessing to everyone she could find, and "many of the Samaritans from that town believed in him because of the woman's testimony" (4:39). What a power she became!

The Next Witnessing Move Is Yours

Take the step. With Christ nothing is impossible. He can give you that miracle life of reproducing yourself, if you'll let Him do it through you. Give the Holy Spirit lots of room to move in your life!

Plenty of Christians don't care! But you can.

You may be saying, "But I'm so weak. Look at my past. Look at my record. Could God possibly use me?"

Yes, absolutely yes!

Or if you say, "But I don't know enough yet!"

You certainly can't tell what you don't know, but you can tell what you do.

The point is, make sure first that *Priority One* is Priority One— that you have given your life over to Jesus Christ to have your

HERMAN

"Try to imagine how much I care!"

Copyright, 1976, Universal Press Syndicate. Reprinted with permission. All rights reserved.

sins totally cleansed away, and that as best you know you've submitted yourself to His Lordship.

Second, remember *Priority Two*, to commit yourself to your fellow Christians. Anyone can do that; you don't need special information or talents. Their fellowship will open your life to new strength and power and resources and authority.

And their support of you and prayer for you will lead you into *Priority Three*: working for Christ and bringing men and women to Him.

God's Only Basic Tool for Witnessing: The Gospel

Jesus to Paul, at the time of his conversion: "Now get up and stand on your feet. I have appeared to you to appoint you as a servant and as a witness of what you have seen of me and what I will show you. . . .

"I am sending you to open their eyes and turn them from darkness to light, and from the power of Satan to God, so that they may receive forgiveness of sins and a place among those who are sanctified by faith in me" (Acts 26:16–18).

God's tool is *not* your life. Your life would never be good enough! "Faith comes from hearing the message, and the message is heard through the word of Christ" (Romans 10:17).

God's tool is *not* your persuasive personality. Paul wrote to the Corinthians, "When I came to you, brothers, I did not come with eloquence or superior wisdom . . . [but] in weakness and fear, and with much trembling" (1 Corinthians 2:1,3).

Then what *does* turn the trick? The gospel itself! "I am not ashamed of the gospel," wrote Paul, "because it is the power of God for the salvation of everyone who believes" (Romans 1:16).

Well, what is the gospel? Paul defines it as a set of facts, when he's talking about his own witnessing:

For what I received I passed on to you as of first importance: that Christ died for our sins according to the Scriptures, that he was buried, that he was raised on the third day according to the Scriptures (1 Corinthians 15:3,4).

You haven't given people the truths which will save them until you've given them these facts about Jesus Christ.

But can you cooperate with the Holy Spirit as you witness of the facts of the gospel? Oh, yes, yes!

Six Traits That Attract

1. *Use good manners,* sensitivity to the feelings of others. Failure to be courteous is failure!

2. *Use good worldly sense.* Seek to know human nature, to get under the other's skin, to have empathy.

3. *Use humor.* Consider yourself part of the problem! A good hearty laugh at yourself deflates the "stuffed shirt" in all of us.

Consecrate your humor; let there be nothing off-color. But sometimes when you witness you'll be awkward. Laughing at yourself will help you both relax.

4. *Use humility.* Constantly deflecting the glory and praise to God in your life will also keep you down off the "soapbox."

5. *Use honesty.* Talk of life's problems. Admitting some of your own will help your friend open up to his own needs.

6. *Use joy,* which is inseparable from the presence of the Holy Spirit!

Increase Your Circle of Love

Some Christians live by this little philosophy:

> We are God's chosen few;
> All the rest are damned.
> There's no room in heaven for you.
> We don't want heaven crammed!

Don't let *that* be your line! Let your heart stretch and grow and grow and stretch.

Your witnessing can't be forever only one-on-one. It must

expand to include the neighborhood, the whole city, your country, your world.

God has in His heart a haunting love for the world, and He wants you to share it with Him.

People, people! How He loves them! All kinds, all colors—all the milling, hurting masses!

I noticed in the Book of Acts His great concern for "the people"—how He kept bringing them into the picture:

> All the people saw him walking and praising God (Acts 3:9);
> All the people were astonished and came running (3:11);
> While they were speaking to the people (4:1);
> Greatly disturbed because the apostles were teaching the people (4:2);
> The people were praising God (4:21);
> Among the people (5:12);
> Highly regarded by the people (5:13);
> Tell the people the full message (5:20).

God loves people! God is concerned for them! And His great concern is that we take this precious gospel which saves and *go to the people.*

We must get the masses of the world on our hearts. We must become "world Christians."

Why do you suppose we're concerned about having concern? Because the masses frighten us. It's hard for us to realize that they're really there, with all their tremendous needs and problems. We'd rather say with the disciples glancing nervously at those five thousand hungry people, "Lord, the time isn't right, the place isn't right, send them away" (*see* Matthew 14:15).

And we don't know them, and masses seem so hard to handle anyway. We feel like the dog chasing the train: "Hey, what am I going to do if I catch it?"

Masses are not a problem to God. All kinds of strategies can work—when we submit ourselves to share His concern.

What if the dog catches the train? In Acts 2:41 three thousand new converts wanted to attach themselves to a hundred and twenty believers. My stars, that sounds like panic time!

Well, together the Christians new and old "devoted themselves" to four things:

1. The apostles' teaching
2. Fellowship
3. Breaking the bread, and
4. Prayer (Acts 2:42).

And in two places:

1. In the temple courts and
2. In their homes (v. 46).

Who could fit in the temple courts? Everyone. Who could fit in homes? Small groups.

And the loving, happy system worked so wonderfully that they continued to add and grow daily (v. 47).

Strategize for the World

1. *You can reach masses by affecting their leaders.*

Maybe you need to go to the president of your company or the mayor of your city and say, "Could I have just three minutes of your time? You have a tremendous job, and I'd love to drop in and pray with you."

Be true to your word and leave on time.

Let me encourage you to go to people who affect people. Be brave, be gutsy!

Elton Trueblood has said, "Whatever else the Lord had in mind, it is clear that He envisioned something very big."

2. *You can reach masses by giving to those who reach the masses.*

Communication is phenomenal today! God can give you discernment to know how and whom to support of those who minister by literature, by radio and television, by schools and hospitals, by Bible translating, by nonmechanical finger-records. . . . The innovations are endless.

The early Christians worked behind the scenes and also took advantage of big public opportunities; they did it all. And out of it all came an atmosphere in the whole society. Faith became the talk of the town. The high priest was saying, "You have filled Jerusalem with your teaching" (Acts 5:28).

John the Baptist's single clapping was becoming a mighty applause!

God gives us special times in our day, when Billy Graham comes to town, or others are on the forefront, and those times can become opportunities to ride in on the waves of popularity and the waves of acceptance.

I don't think that ever before have we had such opportunities as we do today, with such tremendous mobilization of efforts to get the gospel to the whole world. Church and mission agencies are tooling up more and more. Christian, be an involved part of world mission! You live in an exciting day.

3. *You can reach masses by giving yourself to prayer.*

F. B. Meyer and A. B. Simpson were two spiritual giants of the last century. At one time Mr. Meyer was a houseguest in Mr. Simpson's home.

It was early morning, and Meyer thought he was the first one up. He crept downstairs to find a spot to read and pray, and through a door which had been left ajar he saw his host in his study.

He was kneeling before a large world globe, and he would put his finger on a spot and pray. Then he'd spin the globe a little, put his finger on another spot, and pray some more.

And finally as Meyer watched, A. B. Simpson leaned forward and took the whole globe in his arms and began to cry.

Oh, it's a big, hurting world out there! Don't have a little "God bless us four no more" mentality! Who do you know who needs to know the Lord—the hotel doorman down the block? Your own grandmother in a rest home? The desperately poor of North Africa and India?

Right now you need a new *coup d'etat* in your life, a new revolution, to overthrow self now on the throne.

Overthrow your fatness, your love of coddling all that you are and have.

Overthrow your tendency to accumulate rather than to give.

Overthrow your aptness to war rather than to peace.

Overthrow your leaning on self rather than trusting the Spirit.

Overthrow your inertia, your lethargy, your dullness.

Those aren't your problems? Then I'm talking about myself. Lord, give me a new heart for the world!

Anne and I and Nels lived for a while in Afghanistan, when no gospel was allowed among the nationals at all. We had arranged through a friend a secret meeting with one of the most handsome young Afghan men I ever saw.

We sat on the floor with dinner before us in the semidarkness, and through interpretation he began to talk to us:

"I believe in Jesus Christ, and I know that means that before long they'll get me. I understand that. I'm resigned to it. I know that I can never have a girl friend. I can never be married.

"But I have one great longing as a Christian, and I ask you to pray for this. Before they end my life I want to reproduce myself! I want to leave behind me at least one other Afghan Christian.

"Oh, pray for that!"

Questions for Review

1. What is God's one tool for witnessing?
2. What are the facts about Jesus Christ that make up the gospel?
3. What attitudes and qualities can make us winsome witnesses?
4. Discuss the three suggested strategies for witnessing on a wider scale.

TEN

Lord, Teach Me How to Handle My Money

For background, first read Matthew 6:19–34

"Let's go over my sermon again. Surely I must have said something."

Now I'm going to pass on some financial tips to you from the world's greatest Financial Consultant. He's the only One who knows the future, and He guarantees you a fabulous return on your investment. Jesus Christ's advice on any subject is impeccable—including His advice on money. Let me spell out some of His principles.

Principle 1: Money Is for Pleasure

But understand for whose pleasure:

*J*esus

*O*thers

Yourself

Money isn't the root of all evil, only *the love of it is* (1 Timothy 6:10)—the craving for it, the preoccupation with it. That's what will eat you away to nothing inside and make God call you "you fool!" (Luke 12:16–21). That's scary!

Don't accumulate too much of it in its earthly form because it can't buy many of the things you need most.

It can buy recreation, but it can't buy happiness. It can buy a bed, but it can't buy sleep.

It can buy books, but it can't buy wisdom. It can buy "friends," but it can't buy friendships.

It can buy food, but it can't buy an appetite. It can buy a house, but it can't buy a home.

It can buy medicine, but it can't buy health.

Now God still knows you need food, housing, medicine, and so on, and He promises, as you seek Him first, to supply these (Matthew 6:33).

The Ten Commandments show what high value God puts on His children's possessions. One says, "You shall not steal" (Exodus 20:15). Another says, "You shall not covet your neighbor's house . . . your neighbor's wife, or his manservant or his maidservant, his ox or donkey, or anything else that belongs to your neighbor" (Exodus 20:17). "You can't take anyone else's possessions," says God, "because they represent his abilities, his energies, and his time. They belong to him—given by Me."

Another commandment says, "You shall not give false testimony against your neighbor" (Exodus 20:16); you can't take his reputation! Stealing, coveting—these are condemned by God. He protects the things He gives you.

Then He tells you what to do with what He gives you.

Principle 2: Convert Your Gains Quickly to Permanence

> Do not store up for yourselves treasures on earth, where moth and rust destroy, and where thieves break in and steal. But store up for yourselves treasures in heaven, where moth and rust do not destroy, and where thieves do not break in and steal. For where your treasure is, there will your heart be also (Matthew 6:19–21).

If what I am about to tell you sounds like secular advice, God said it first. You must not only work for money, but your money must work for you. In this way your net worth will be continually increasing. How do you do it?

Convert a hefty part of your assets. Transfer it, on at least a weekly basis, from the now to the hereafter. Right in this life—in fact, only in this life—you can do it! You can't buy your way to heaven, and yet amazingly, God lets you pay for Christian work to be done that others may hear how to get there. He wants you to convert your concrete dollars into spiritual activity.

The Apostle Paul wrote to his young pastor-friend Timothy:

Command those who are rich in this present world not to be arrogant nor to put their hope in wealth, which is so uncertain, but to put their hope in God, who richly provides us with everything for our enjoyment. Command them to do good, to be rich in good deeds, and to be generous and willing to share.

In this way they will lay up treasure for themselves as a firm foundation for the coming age, so that they may take hold of the life that is truly life (1 Timothy 6:17–19).

Did you notice in Matthew 6:19–21 it says "for yourselves," "for yourselves"? And here in Timothy "for themselves"? This is for you, Christian! This is *your* money, permanently stored away in heaven *for you.*

You may put into an offering plate ten dollars, a hundred dollars, a thousand dollars, who knows? And in your mind's eye you see it flying away—money with wings on it—and you think, *Well, I'll never see that again.* Oh, no! *That's the only money you will see again!* It's being credited to your account. *The Living Bible* paraphrases 1 Timothy 6:19 this way:

By doing this they will be storing up real treasure for themselves in heaven—it is the only safe investment for eternity! And they will be living a fruitful Christian life down here as well.

Principle 3: Use It or Lose It

Everything you are and have that you don't make to work properly, you lose.

A singer who quits singing soon can't sing. A typist who no longer types soon can't type. Use it or lose it.

Money is the same: invest it according to certain principles or it's gone.

Around 450 B.C. the Israelites' temple to the Lord was in great need of repair, and they hadn't roused themselves to do anything about it. *Yet they themselves lived in nice houses.* Here's a clear-cut case of when possessing didn't pay.

"You expected much, but see, it turned out to be little. What you brought home, I blew away. Why?" declares the Lord Almighty. "Because of my house, which remains a ruin, while each of you is busy with his own house" (Haggai 1:9).

You see, instead of escaping poverty by not giving, they actually increased it. They would not give to God what they could have given Him, so God blew upon their money; He blasted it; He blighted it.

The problem with the Israelites was *priority.* The house of God, the special place where He would meet with them, wasn't central in their lives.

Their sin was a sin of omission. You know, it's easy to rationalize! "It's not time to build the house of the Lord. We haven't yet recovered from the exile. We are economically unsound. We have to be careful! Yes, we know you must live by faith, but you have to have good common sense, too."

Or maybe they said, "These are recession days. They're hard times. We can't build yet." Or, "It's this inflation that's killing us. Taxes. Rising cost of living."

So the chairman of the building committee said, "Let's wait. Then we can do a really good job later on. All in favor say 'aye.' "

"Aye."

"Aye."

"Aye."

Everybody voted yes, and the house of God went unfinished.

One of the commentators on Haggai says:

"Looks like the pastor has found a way to motivate the building committee."

They had thought that their bad season necessarily caused delay of their duty, but really it was their delay that was causing the bad season.

A contemporary translation might go like this:
"You think that your unexpected bills necessarily caused delay of your giving to the work of Christ—but really it is your

delay of your giving to the work of Christ that is causing your unexpected bills."

One Christian was thinking about God's blowing on the Israelites' money and he said, "You know, Philippians 4:18 says that a gift to God is a fragrant offering, pleasing to Him. I think when we give to Him He inhales; He enjoys the sweet smell. And when we withhold, He exhales. He blows on what we have, and away it goes."

When a great tycoon of Wall Street died, someone asked, "How much did he leave?" And the reply was, "He left it all."

Principle 4: Give—to Get—to Give

One of England's famous Christians awhile back was Robert Laidlaw, who always kept a diary.

When he was eighteen he wrote, "Wages, three dollars per week. I have decided to start giving one tenth to the Lord."

When he was twenty he wrote:

Before money gets a grip on my heart, by the grace of God I enter into the following pledge with my Lord:
That I will give 10 percent of all I earn up to—(so much).
If the Lord blesses me with (so much more) I will give 15 percent of all I earn.
And if the Lord blesses me with (a higher amount), I will give 20 percent of all I earn.
If the Lord blesses me with (even more) I will give 25 percent of all I earn.

Then he added this prayer: "Lord, help me to keep this promise for Christ's sake, who gave all for me." And he signed his name to it.

When he was twenty-five he wrote, "I have decided to change the above graduated scale, and start now giving 50 percent of all my earnings."

Many years later, in 1961, Robert Laidlaw testified that God had skyrocketed his income all through the years, and he'd been able to give more than he ever dreamed.

Christian, if you will give as God directs, He will give to you—so that you can give more.

> Give, and it will be given to you. A good measure, pressed down, shaken together and running over, will be poured into your lap [no purse or checkbook big enough]. For with the measure you use, it will be measured to you (Luke 6:38).

(Someone asked me once, "Pastor Ray, should I tithe my net income or my gross?" And I asked back, "Do you want to be blessed on the net or on the gross?")

Now here is the clear word of Christ. 2 Corinthians 9:10,11 spells out even further what your return is for:

> Now he who supplies seed to the sower and bread for food will also supply and increase your store of seed and will enlarge the harvest of your righteousness. You will be made rich in every way so that you can be generous on every occasion, and through us your generosity will result in thanksgiving to God.

When you want to be a channel for God's funds, God will see that you get the funds so that you *can* be. He won't give so that you can live lavishly and do whatever you want. Don't fall for the preachers today who feed you the line, "God wants you to be well and rich!" That's just not in the Bible, and even the great Paul was neither well nor rich!

But give more of that which is given to you, and even more will be given to you, so that you can give even more! That's the point.

We all love Philippians 4:19: "And my God will meet all your needs according to his glorious riches in Christ Jesus." We quote it a lot. But what's the context of that verse? Paul was in prison, and the Christians in Philippi regularly, generously sent him money and supplies. Paul wrote this letter as a "thank you," and he said, "I am amply supplied, now that I have received from Epaphroditus the gifts you sent. . . . And my God will meet all your needs. . . ."

That verse says that if you have given faithfully, your own needs will be abundantly supplied. God will not let you go wanting, but He'll give back to meet your own needs and to allow you to give more.

Principle 5: You Can Never Give Too Much

Jesus sat down opposite the place where the offerings were put and watched the crowd putting their money into the temple treasury. Many rich people threw in large amounts. But a poor widow came and put in two very small copper coins, worth only a fraction of a penny.

Calling his disciples to him, Jesus said, "I tell you the truth, this poor widow has put more into the treasury than all the others. They all gave out of their wealth; but she, out of her poverty, put in everything—all she had to live on" (Mark 12:41–44).

Now this woman (not a man, a wage earner in those days, but a woman—even a widow; get the picture?) had two coins, and she could have given one of the two. That would have been 50 percent; not bad giving! But she gave both of her coins, everything she possessed.

I wonder if the disciples said, "Lord, you won't let her do it, will you? Make her take it back." But Jesus not only let her do it, He praised her for it.

Why? Because all the rest of Scripture would honor her as a godly martyr who starved to death? Not at all! Because a rich uncle was about to die and she would immediately become wealthy? No! But the Scriptures all testify that God would take abundant care of her, in His own way. God's just ones "shall live by faith." It's the lifestyle He requires of us for blessing.

This woman is representative of God's attitude toward giving. Jesus doesn't say either that she'll starve or get rich; He simply leaves her to God, and He knows what God would do.

But by this incident He says loudly and clearly that you can never give too much. You simply cannot. You'll never go to heaven and say, "Why did I give so much to the Lord's work? I could have really lived high." You'll never have that thought. You'll say, "Why didn't I love more? Why didn't I give more? Why didn't I care more?"

You can't give too much.

Principle 6: Give Proportionately to Your Income

I realize this is definitely a step down from the widow's giving! But Jesus uses her as the great example and then gets on to the rest of us.

God based giving under the Old Testament Laws on a tithe—ten percent—and then commanded His people to give offerings, about another ten percent; so when all was done the Jews gave about twenty percent or more. We must be fair and realize that this money also cared for their government expenses.

But how earnestly God looked on to see if they were faithful to what He had required of them! He made sure they understood that those tithes and offerings were His, not theirs; and when they withheld, He asked:

Will a man rob God? Yet you rob me.
But you ask, "How do we rob you?"
In tithes and offerings. You are under a curse—the whole nation of you—because you are robbing me (Malachi 3:8,9).

Well, how were they to repent from this?

"Bring the whole tithe into the storehouse, that there may be food in my house. Test me in this," says the Lord Almighty, "and see if I will not throw open the floodgates of heaven and pour out so much blessing that you will not have room enough for it" (verse 10).

The New Testament continues the principle of percentage giving. In Matthew 23:23 Jesus said that they were getting picky about the details of it, and yet they were still right to do it!

From here on you don't read anything specifically about tithing. But there's a command running through it all that's far more than ten percent in attitude! You just don't find that calculating, mathematical spirit in the rest of the New Testament.

1 Corinthians 16:2 spells out proportionate giving:

On the first day of every week [He tells them when; on Sundays bring your offerings together]

Each one of you [nobody's left out; He wants 100 percent giving]

Should set aside a sum of money in keeping with his income. . . .

There's percentage giving. As you make more, give more. I'm sure you wouldn't give less than an Old Testament Jew—not under grace! A tithe is just the beginning.

Three Advantages of Proportionate Giving

1. If you write out that first check from your income to the Lord, you'll probably treat all the rest of your possessions as more sacred before Him. You'll be careful with all of it; it could have that effect on your life.

2. When you tithe week by week, you'll shift more funds to your heavenly account than you ever did before. Obey God's

command "on the first day of the week." Don't write monthly checks. You may say, "I get paid once a month or twice a month; why should I give to the Lord more often than I get a paycheck?" Out of obedience to the Lord. Why argue with Him?

3. Tithing is a preventative against depression. Let me tell you why. When you've been faithful to God in your tithes and offerings, and financial tough times come, you don't get depressed. You say, "You know, Lord, that I've been faithful. I've been trying to handle my money as You tell me to, so I know You'll see me through." And you'll have a sense of victory.

I know a young husband who was just getting started in life, with a modest little home, a wife, and a couple of babies. He and his wife were brand-new Christians. One Sunday they were about to take off for Sunday school and church and were flying around cleaning up the kitchen because they were having company after church—

. . . and the sink stopped up.

Dennis just looked up to heaven in despair and bellowed, "God, I tithed!"

Immediately the drain went s-l-lur-urp!—and the sink worked fine again!

I can't promise that will always happen!

Principle 7: Give Voluntarily and With Joy

2 Corinthians 8 and 9 are great chapters on giving. Here Paul uses the poverty-stricken Christians of Macedonia as the shining example for the rest of us. They loved to give! Says Paul:

> For I testify that they gave as much as they were able, and even beyond their ability. Entirely on their own . . . (8:3).

(God's not ever going to twist your arm.)

... they urgently pleaded with us for the privilege of sharing in this service to the saints. And they did not do so as we expected, but they gave themselves first to the Lord and then to us in keeping with God's will (8:4,5).

(God's will was first, Priority One—giving themselves to God; and second, Priority Two—giving themselves even with their money to their brothers and sisters in Christ.)

Remember this: whoever sows sparingly will also reap sparingly, and whoever sows generously will also reap generously. Each man should give what he has decided in his heart to give, not reluctantly or under compulsion, for God loves a cheerful giver (2 Corinthians 9:6,7).

You may be a little unhappy here because I give a section of this book to talking about money. Maybe you even think that an all-out-for-God kind of Christian living might not be any fun because it might take so much of your money. Well, depend on the Lord: it's one of His miracles that giving produces joy, that more giving produces more joy, and that absolutely reckless giving produces hilarious joy! ("Hilarious" is God's word for it in 2 Corinthians 9:7!)

I am truly telling you the way to be happy. You won't believe it until you test Him.

I'm doing you a favor! Every new Christian needs to be told at the beginning that his life of faith will prosper more through trusting God with his money than in probably any other area. That's why one-sixth of the entire New Testament is about your possessions. If any minister wanted to be faithful to emphasize in exact proportion that which the Bible emphasizes, he'd have to preach one sermon out of every six on possessions.

On the other hand, there's Jesus' own preaching: *almost one-half of His parables were about money!*

And I'm doing you a favor because if you give, you'll get. No, I'm not telling you to give so you'll get rich. I'm talking about giving so that you'll have more to give. The minute you settle down in your riches and become one of the "fat cats"—I tell you, God will not give you any more of it. Or He'll not bless you for it.

In a world so needy, God can't afford to bless hoarders—that is, those who hoard their money down here. Hoard up your money in heaven! Release it here—to hoard it there.

Anyone who on this earth merely feeds upon himself, who turns inward on himself and squanders his time and attention on himself—he dies inside.

But when you give yourself away, you're released. You're renewed. You have freshness. Your capacity to love expands. You feel good toward God. Love acts! Love moves! Jesus says if you're going to give and live in life, you must be in gear, you must go, you must move, you must invest, you must give yourself.

You've taken care of the needs of others and wonder of wonders!—you've also taken care of yourself. You've banked every dime of it in your personal account in heaven. It will be there waiting for you—to your amazement, to your joy!

And remember this:

No way does God ever need your money. He says:

> I have no need of a bull from your stall
>   or of goats from your pens,
> for every animal of the forest is mine
>   and the cattle on a thousand hills.
> I know every bird in the mountains,
>   and the creatures of the field are mine.
> If I were hungry I would not tell you,
>   for the world is mine, and all that is
>   in it (Psalm 50:9–12).

He is the only source of it all, and He distributes it as He pleases.

He doesn't need your money, but *you need to give.* It's the way you learn to trust Him, to prove true His promises to provide for you.

It's a tangible, obvious way you learn obedience. Daniel Webster said, "One of the most awesome things in all the world is my accountability to Almighty God."

> Shortly after the fall of France, a Frenchman wrote an American, "We came to imagine that the proper duty of men was to arrange an easy way of life, individualistic to the point of selfishness. . . . We looked upon the state as a universal purveyor, and we always spoke of our due, seldom of our duties. . . .
>
> "Tell all this to the Americans, and warn them of the peril that may befall democracy everywhere when it forgets that free men have duties as well as rights."

I asked an athletic trainer of young men what advice he'd give to young Christians for this book, or to Christians who wanted to be renewed. He said, "Three things.

"One, give God your time. He must be Lord over each day's schedule, so there's time for study and prayer.

"Two, give God your reputation. If you don't you'll never witness; you'll never have the courage to get out there where it counts.

"Three, give God your finances. If you don't let go of that, you'll be personally unhealthy and divided. 'You cannot serve both God and money'—Matthew 6:24."

Principle 8: Give to God and Not to Men

When you give you're not "investing," in the stock market sense.

This is important!

When you invest in a business, you have every right to know just how your money's being used. They're accountable to you, and you can call them on the carpet for mismanagement.

There is no parallel that I know of in Scripture to this situation. If you think you're giving to a Christian church or cause as if it were a company, you'll demand an accounting of every penny, and you'll withhold funds if the money doesn't go where you please. These days this kind of mind-set has done a lot of damage.

When Christians in the Book of Acts gave their money there seemed to be a relaxed spirit of trust. They simply "put it at the apostles' feet" (Acts 4:35).

The givers were accountable *only to God*, not to men, and they were accountable only to give the amounts that He directed and with cheerful hearts.

Then the receivers of that money were also accountable *only to God,* not to men; and they were accountable to disperse it in obedience to Him and of course for the purpose it was intended.

Of course you want to be careful to ask God for wisdom to give to Him through the proper channels—your church, other Christian causes. If indeed you just can't support your church at all, then you need to go to a church that you can support!

But the bottom line is, don't give your money to men. Then you'd always be checking to see if they "deserve" it.

Give it cheerfully and freely to God!

The Holy Spirit is nudging you not only to hear the truth but to do it. If your spouse, family, or another is involved, answer this question together: what percentage of my/our income(s) shall I/we give to God, starting now?

_____ %

Questions for Review

1. What is the assurance we have, according to Philippians 4:19, if we give faithfully to the Lord?
2. What is a tithe?
3. What is proportionate giving? Where in the New Testament is this taught?
4. If God doesn't need what we have to give, why does He place so much emphasis on the subject?

ELEVEN

Lord, Keep Me Growing

For background, first read Acts 7:17–38

I was jogging on my favorite beach awhile back, and I stopped to watch some sandpipers. Those little birds are like pint-sized gulls that flock on the wet sand at the water's edge.

When a wave washed out they'd run out in a little group, pecking for tiny creatures to eat. When a wave washed in they'd come running back on their spindly little legs; and then when the wave receded they'd run-run-run out again, pecking for goodies; and then run-run-run back with the next wave. . . . And then run-run-run out, and then run-run-run in. . . .

All except one. There was one little fellow that never could catch up, and I realized he had only one leg. He would go hop,

hop out, to get at least one peck, but before he could get very far, here would come a wave and he'd have to hop, hop back. Sometimes he'd nearly get swamped, but when the wave receded he'd hop, hop out again.

I watched and I thought, *You know he's really quite a little guy. He relentlessly keeps at it. They feast while he fasts, but he doesn't give up.*

I jogged on down the beach and when I came back there he was, still keeping at it. Hopping out. Hopping back. Probably not getting a whole lot.

And he was sort of frumpier than the others; he didn't have a lot of class. But he really captured my heart, and I found myself cheering him on: "Come on, little guy! Make it, make it! Find something, you can do it!"

There was a day when he lost that leg, and he didn't lie down and die. He said, "Well, it's not much fun this way, but I'm going to keep on. I'll do the best I can."

He had my vote for being the Number One Sandpiper on the beach. I think City Hall should declare a day in honor of one-legged sandpipers, and give them a little encouragement and recognition.

Sooner or later all of us Christians feel like one-legged sandpipers. We feel we're frumpy when others are sleek. We remember yesterdays when we were wounded and we think, *Nobody hurts the way I hurt.* We hop; others run. They get the good stuff; we get very little.

Look with me at the life of Moses.

Moses, back in the Book of Exodus, felt himself to be a one-legged sandpiper. He had an inferiority complex that just about paralyzed him, and yet he grew into one of the great leaders of all world history.

You want to grow and keep growing?

Moses' Life: Phase One

Moses, even more than most of us, was born into a cruel, complex world. His people the Jews were hostages in Egypt, and you read in Exodus 1:11 and following that Egyptian slave masters forced them to build huge cities for them under terrible conditions.

Anne and I were in this very area recently looking at ruins of some of the very brick buildings these Hebrews constructed, and we couldn't believe the relentless heat and the relentless flies and the relentless oppressiveness of the air. For us there was the escape of a plane that would lift us out of that searing, baking desert and take us away. But for the Hebrews there was no escape.

Moses was born to two of these slaves whose multiplying was so threatening to the Egyptians. And right then Pharaoh had reached his limit:

> Pharaoh gave this order to all his people: "Every boy that is born you must throw into the river, but let every girl live" (Exodus 1:22).

So Baby Moses was born with a death sentence upon his tiny head.

When any baby is born he moves from womb security and comfort to drafts and loud noises and sudden lights and being lifted around and having to eat for himself; it must be quite a shock. But in addition to all that, how do you suppose newborn Moses felt? Did he begin to sense the panic of his parents, who knew that soon his little body was to be drowned in the river?

Exodus is the name of Moses' book, and *exodus* means "out of." God came to the rescue! He lifted Baby Moses *out of* that terrible situation, just as, through Moses, He would soon lift all the Hebrews *out of* the land of Egypt.

In a sense God was saying, "Pharaoh, I laugh at your attempts to thwart Me. I will turn your very schemes against you. Your own daughter will rescue a Hebrew babe from the river, and you'll raise him as an adopted son in your own family. You will finance his whole upbringing. You will pay his mother to raise him, and you will educate him and teach him all the wisdom of the Egyptians; and then when he's mature he will lead all your millions of Hebrew slaves to escape from under your cruel hand."

Believer, the longer you live as a Christian, the more you'll realize your life story could be called Exodus! God will rescue you over and over—pulling you out of terrible situations in the nick of time. *Relax in advance; He will never fail to take care of you.*

So Moses grew up in the palace of Pharaoh, thoroughly trained in the courts of the world's ruling power in its days of the glory of pyramids and mathematics, "educated in all the wisdom of the Egyptians" (Acts 7:22). Some upbringing! By the age of forty he was still unmarried, pampered, and apparently immature.

But God wasn't through with him yet.

Nor is He through with you.

Moses' Life: Phase Two

When God is committed to a person's growth, what does He do? Well, He creates some new circumstances—a jolt here, some pressure there—to get him out of his comfortable rut.

> One day, after Moses had grown up, he went out to where his own people were and watched them at their hard labor (Exodus 2:11).

Watching them, he probably felt guilty that he, a fellow Hebrew, had it so good. Maybe for the first time he felt his heart tugging toward them as they struggled and sweat and were abused there in that unrelieving desert sun.

"He saw an Egyptian beating a Hebrew, one of his own people. Glancing this way and that and seeing no one, he killed the Egyptian and hid him in the sand.

"The next day he went out and saw two Hebrews fighting. He

asked the one in the wrong, 'Why are you hitting your fellow Hebrew?'

"The man said, 'Who made you ruler and judge over us? Are you thinking of killing me as you killed the Egyptian?'

"Then Moses was afraid and thought, 'What I did must have become known.'

"When Pharaoh heard of this, he tried to kill Moses, but Moses fled from Pharaoh and went to live in Midian, where he sat down by a well" (Exodus 2:11–15).

> Moses had spent forty years thinking he was somebody.
>
> Now he was going to spend the next forty years discovering that he was nobody.
>
> But after that he would live the last forty years experiencing what God can do with a nobody!

In Midian (*whoever heard of Midian?*) from ages forty to eighty, Moses raised a family and herded smelly sheep. (In Egypt, herding sheep had been considered the most detestable occupation of all—Genesis 46:34.)

He had all his "good years," supposedly, to chew over the fact that he'd started out life with fantastic privileges, and he'd blown the whole thing.

He was a has-been.

He was a loser.

And God didn't cut short this lesson. He let Moses get the picture thoroughly in his head for forty years!

Career-wise, Moses was trapped. He had all the mathematical and scientific skills of the great Egypt, all the personnel and governmental knowledge of the world's ruling country—but to use all that he had to go back to Egypt itself, and Egypt was where he couldn't go.

He was so unprepared for everyday living outside the palace that by the age of eighty, he was still just tending the sheep of his father-in-law; he apparently never managed to build up a flock of his own! Maybe his wife and sons despised him as much as he despised himself.

"One-legged sandpiper?" Moses would say to us. "I'm not even that. I'm a total paraplegic!"

That's how we find him in Exodus 3:1. He'd been prepared to be Top Drawer, and then he'd spent his career getting sun-scorched and calloused from work for which he was unfit.

Guindon

"*Another reason I won't go out with you, Harvey, is that you have such a low opinion of yourself.*"

Guindon © 1981, Los Angeles Times Syndicate. Reprinted with permission.

He's broken. He's whipped.

And he's eighty years old. It's all over.

(*Anything in your own life that makes you identify here? There is in mine. Well, let's keep going.*)

Moses' Life: Phase Three

A fire is burning. A bush in the desert is on fire, and it doesn't seem to burn up.

Moses goes over to investigate—and you can read the details in Exodus 3. God is invading the life of this broken man. It's time for him to grow some more! And God comes in miracle and glory—*and He will come to your life,* sometimes when you least expect Him.

God appears at Horeb, the mountain of God, also called Sinai. How could Moses know that this mountain, along with Calvary and Zion, would become a trio of mountains for God's eternal strategies?

Moses had just moved out of the realm of smelly sheep and hot sun and into the realm of God! The place where he stood would soon be the site of—

God's miracle-provisions of care (Exodus 17:6); His very presence among His people and His giving of the law (Exodus 19,20); His one-on-one meetings with two special men, Moses and Elijah (Exodus 33:21–23 and 1 Kings 19:11–13), maybe in the same cleft of the same rock; the outrageous rebellion of multitudes (Exodus 32:1–35) and their repentance (Exodus 33:4–6).

God even reassured Moses at this point: "Moses, I'll give a sign that I'm for real: when you have led the Hebrews out of Egypt, you will worship me on this very same mountain" (*see* v. 12).

But how could Moses dream that it would be with thunder, lightning, thick clouds, trumpet blasts, smoke, and earthquakes (Exodus 19:16–20)?

God introduced Himself to Moses as

"The God of Abraham,

Isaac,

and Jacob."

Abraham: an idolator (Joshua 24:2).

His son Isaac—sort of a "nobody."

His grandson Jacob: a

downright schemer and thief.

God: *"I am the God of*

pagans,

nobodies,

and thieves.

"I am the same One now calling you,

Moses!"

Or how could he guess God would there write on stone tablets with His own finger, and give them to Moses to carry in his own hands (Exodus 31:18)?

Or how could Moses envision that he would lead up his brother and nephews and seventy Hebrew elders and they would *see God*?

That under God's feet there would be like a pavement made of sapphire or lapis lazuli, clear as the sky itself—

And that these seventy-four men would eat and drink in the presence of God—

And not even fall dead (Exodus 24:9–11)!

Moses was just tending his sheep—and just that suddenly, he was into Big Time! Had Moses moved, to make it happen? No, God, on His own sovereign schedule, came to where Moses was.

Friend, look to God to do the moving, the arranging, the working out deals in your life to make you grow. He's committed to that! Learn to walk by faith (2 Corinthians 5:7). Keep "tending your sheep," but keep your eyes open for His surprise moves of miracle and power.

Maybe today!

But if forty years from now—still "wait for the Lord. Be strong and take heart and wait for the Lord" (Psalm 27:14).

If you don't learn anything else as a new Christian, learn to walk each day by faith. Do your daily duties as best you can, but keep your eyes up. Expect the supernatural to keep breaking through to you. You're not just anybody's child—you're a child of God! He will care for you and work for you, with all His infinite resources and power.

God always works in the principle of miracle. Through a bush that never burned up God was introducing Moses to the fact that from now on he would live on a miracle basis.

I've prayed many times, and I know when I prayed it for the first time, "Lord, make my life a miracle! Give me a ministry that can only be explained on the basis that God is in it—not on the basis of any other thing—that Ray Ortlund had the right breaks, or his church happened to be on a good corner, or anything else. It has to be explainable only by the fact that God Himself is pulling it off! Lord, make my life a miracle!"

So from age eighty to a hundred and twenty, Moses is going to live a miracle life.

Don't think people were so weird back then that they all did their best work at a hundred and twenty. Moses wrote in the Ninetieth Psalm, "The length of our days is seventy years—or eighty, if we have the strength. . . ."

No, God was going to give him a miracle ministry, and even when he died "his eyes were not weak nor his strength gone" (Deuteronomy 34:7).

And Christian, God will give you every resource for everything He ever wants you to do for Him—forever!

And God didn't pick Moses because He could see that Moses was potentially some giant.

An unforgettable experience. An undeniable call. God doesn't say, "Please try going to Pharaoh, Moses. Give it your best shot. Let's see if it works." No way. In His voice of majesty in fire He says, "*When you have brought the people out of Egypt, you will worship me here.*"

Ethel Waters used to say, "God don't sponsor no flops!" His commands are all the assurance we need.

But Moses wasn't assured at all! He still had an inferiority complex as tall as Mount Horeb! His response was, "Who am I, that I should go . . . ?" (Exodus 3:11).

"Who am I?" was the wrong question. But then he asked the right one: "Who are you?" (v. 13).

Everything depends on who God really is.

God's answer was mysterious, phenomenal:

> "I AM WHO I AM,
> THAT IS MY NAME."

Almost seven thousand times this name of God is used in the Old Testament. Yahweh. Jehovah. The Hebrew word for "to be."

It simply means GOD IS—and if you really know that, it's enough. He is your wisdom, your love, your comfort, your provisions, your guidance, your righteousness—He's everything for you.

That's why getting to know the Lord, deeply and well, has got to be Priority One, your life's most important project. This is how you'll grow and keep growing! Everything else depends on that: every attitude, every relationship, every vision, every achievement. All God's great men have been ordinary men who came to know Him and count on Him.

Moses was overwhelmed by his inadequacies. Because he didn't really know yet who God was, he was full of anxieties over who he, Moses, was. He thought God needed the help of somebody "big deal" to accomplish this thing with Pharaoh! Now, Pharaoh was really "big deal," and to Moses, obviously God couldn't change Pharaoh all by Himself, so He needed a "partner" for the project who was in the league of Pharaoh.

But Moses? Moses was from a minority race, a slave class; he had murdered; and for the last forty years he'd been a disgusting *shepherd.* "Who am I, that I should go?"

But God chooses "the weak things of the world to shame the strong . . . so that no one may boast before him" (1 Corinthians 1:27–29).

Christian, do you feel disqualified for greatness? Then let me read you a letter I just received.

Dear Pastor Ray,

I have waited nearly five years now for this day when I would locate you and tell you of the wonderful blessings that the Lord has bestowed upon me and how you were instrumental in helping to make His will a reality in my life.

In November of 1977 I wrote to you and told you how God had put me in prison for bank robbery during a suicidal attempt. This had followed ten years of hospitalizations for various attempts. [I do remember her—that she told me she had finally robbed a bank in desperation, hoping that in the act she would get shot and killed. She didn't, and she went to prison.]

I told you that I had accepted Jesus as my Lord while in prison and how it was the best thing that had ever happened to me.

You sent me a letter, one page thanking me and you said that God had great things planned for me, to hang in there and let Him do it. I placed this letter in a frame and hung it on the wall of my cell. Whenever I would get discouraged I would read your letter and give the pressure to Jesus. Yes, He took it and He proved it true. . . .

[After I got out of prison] I wanted to return to school and become a social worker so that I could serve God. He allowed this to happen. In September 1980 I graduated from _____ with Honors and was listed in the National Dean's List for high academic achievement. I went directly into a graduate school of social work at _____ where I just graduated with a master's degree in social work. Now I am seeking work in a Christian organization where I can use my knowledge and skills to serve the Lord.

I take little credit for the accomplishments I have made in these past years. I owe it all to Jesus. Without His precious blood and His undying love for me I never would have made it. I am certain that the Holy Spirit wrote my thesis for me when I was too exhausted to do it myself. My love for God has grown stronger and stronger. I feel His presence always and I know that He helps me with every detail.

What I once thought was impossible, what the psychiatrists, psychologists, social workers, prosecutors, and others thought impossible, unrealistic, has become a reality and possible through faith in God. *I hope to use this miracle to bless others who doubt that those who suffer from emotional problems can ever lead normal lives. It is possible when you give your life to Jesus. . . .*

Christian, believe that totally right now, and grow a little.

You see, the key is God Himself. "I will be with you," He says.

He seeks to build into you confidence—even excited anticipation over what He will do with you!

Plenty of believers (and plenty of churches) never get out there on the cutting edge, out where it's dangerous and risky, because they say, "Who am *I* . . . ?" "Who are *we* . . . ?"

But those questions have nothing to do with it. All God has to work with are sinners and failures. That's all there are!

But Moses' fears died hard. "What if they do not believe me?" (Exodus 4:1).

More miracles are performed. "The constantly burning bush was not enough? All right, I give you a rod that turns into a snake, that turns into a rod again. I give you a healthy hand that turns leprous, that turns into a healthy hand again."

"This," says the Lord, "is so that they may believe . . ." (v. 5). (How kind He is! He also means, "so that *you* may believe, Moses.")

"But, Lord," interrupts Moses, going back to Argument One: "I have never been eloquent . . . I am slow of speech."

Many feel that Moses' problem was stuttering. "L-l-lord, I c-c-can't speak for you; I s-s-s-stutter."

The Lord didn't answer, "Oh, I didn't realize! Thank you for telling Me, Moses; 'scuse me, I'll pick somebody else."

No, His answer is more like thundering, "Well, then *stutter for me, Moses!*"

He actually answered him with one of the most amazing statements of Scripture:

> Who gave man his mouth? Who makes him deaf or dumb? Who gives him sight or makes him blind? Is it not I, the Lord? (v. 11).

But Moses still refuses: "Lord, let somebody else do it."

And finally God's anger burns, and He appoints Moses' brother Aaron to be the front man, the mouthpiece for Moses' leadership.

Plan B instead of Plan A? "Moses, *you will go,* if not first class then second class, because I have decreed it."

"God leads his dear children along," Bob Pierce of World Vision used to say, "but me He has to yank." That's true with many of us, isn't it?

Well, Moses complains some more, and in Exodus 6 God gives him the strongest commands and promises yet:

"I am the Lord. . . .

"I appeared. . . .

"I made promises. . . .

"I will bring you out. . . .

"I will take you. . . .

"Then you will know. . . .

"I am the Lord."

From that magnificent speech Moses crept out and said something (through Aaron) to the Hebrews; they didn't listen, and he was more discouraged than ever.

And *at that critical time* God said to him, "Go tell Pharaoh to let my people go."

"LORD!" Moses howled. "If the Israelites don't listen, why would Pharaoh"—and he couldn't resist—"since I s-s-s-stutter?"

the neighborhood™ Jerry Van Amerongen

"You're not a good loser, Gene . . ."

Reprinted courtesy The Register and Tribune Syndicate, Inc.

Isn't this ridiculous? God had already substituted Aaron to do the talking.

Does it seem as if the story is needlessly dragging out? Well, that's the way an inferiority complex can cripple you, embarrass you, discourage you—year after year, through adolescence, through young adulthood, through middle age, and into old age—with no seeming relief at all.

We have the same old baloney again in Exodus 6:30: "But Moses said to the Lord, 'Since I speak with faltering lips, why would Pharaoh listen to me?' "

Moses! We settled that issue! What are you doing, whining over it again?

Well, Moses was a one-legged sandpiper, but God just kept after him until he was willing to go stand in the court of Pharaoh.

It wasn't the same Pharaoh who'd adopted him eighty years before, but one just as bad; he was still bitterly oppressing his Hebrew slaves. He was a man who was powerful, cruel, and greatly feared.

And Moses is supposed to go make this huge demand of him?

A one-legged sandpiper stands out in a crowd anyway, just because he's so frumpy and pathetic-looking. A poor self-image is embarrassingly obvious to everybody.

You wonder if they're all despising you.

You don't dare smile because maybe you've still got some breakfast on your teeth.

And whatever's required of you at the moment—will you be up to it? Probably not. You'll botch it up terribly, and they'll still be remembering it ten years from now.

But the only requirement was obedience. And—

By George, into Pharaoh's awesome presence come two Hebrew brothers, ages eighty and eighty-three—and one of them a *shepherd!*

YEA, MOSES! You made it! You did it! You got there!

And from that ridiculous little moment of obedience on, miracles began to pour forth.

Staffs became snakes!

Frogs multiplied and disappeared on command!

So did flies and boils and hail and locusts!

And deep darkness covered all of Egypt except for the bright, sunny spot where the Israelites lived. How could you explain that?

And before long several million Israelites were openly marching out of the country of Egypt—after the Egyptians, as if mesmerized, had loaded them down with all their personal jewelry and clothing! (Besides—are you ready for this?—the Big Plunder had been prophesied about five hundred years before [Genesis 15:13,14]!)

So God was "growing up" His servant. And over the following years Moses logged in lots of time with God.

Listen, *there is no substitute for time with God.* If you're a new Christian, maybe even by reading this book you're saying, "I want to be a spiritual giant in a hurry!" Look, you have to log up time with God.

Moses had one experience with God after another: The Red Sea crossing, water from a rock, complaining followers, manna, quail—so many lessons to be learned!

God was growing him up, as God wants to grow you up.

Maturity Will Come

Forty years have passed and Aaron, Moses' spokesman, finally dies (Numbers 33:39). Now would Moses retreat into his shell?

No way! He had grown up! He'd come to know God well— and therefore he could forget himself.

> And the entire Book of Deuteronomy—can you believe this!—is a compilation of all the speeches Moses made after Aaron died, all by himself!

Moses is up in front of everybody in Deuteronomy 32:1:

L-l-l-listen, O heavens, and I will s-s-s-speak; Hear, O earth, the w-w-words of my mouth!

But, Moses, you stutter!
"I don't care."

You said you weren't eloquent!

"God doesn't mind!—But ex-s-s-scuse me, I'm addressing the Israelites:

> 'Let my teaching fall like rain,
> And my words descend like d-d-d-dew. . . .' "

ATTA BOY, MOSES!

You've grown up. You've learned what God is like, and now you live trusting Him.

I was born into a Swedish-American home in Des Moines, Iowa. I was the last of five children, and we only had a three-bedroom house. I'm sure I was a surprise.

All my boyhood I went next door to sleep in my aunt's home, and I remember feeling, "I'm the one who has to disappear at bedtime because I don't fit in this family."

They were good people; they didn't mean to give this message at all. But I remember the words I heard, running after the big guys whom I adored: "Hey, Ray, go home. Hey, dummy, what's the matter with you?"

I heard the word *dummy* over and over, and I believed it. Now, they didn't mean anything by it; it was just kids' rhetoric in the neighborhood, that's all. Theoretically I knew I was loved. But I grew up with words inside me, "Hey, Ray, you dummy."

I did poorly in school. I had a hard time with myself.

Then God gave me a friend, a wonderful friend. Eventually I married her. I remember at the beginning of our honeymoon, traveling from Washington, D.C., to the Shenandoah Valley in Virginia, I shared with her my doubts, my troubles, my feelings of insecurity. They were very deep. I felt like that one-legged sandpiper, and I told her about it.

And from then on I just shared these things with her. I don't think I'd ever shared them with anyone else before.

Sometimes she'd say, "Ray, that's your imagination. What you're feeling isn't reality at all," and she'd affirm me.

Sometimes she'd say, "You're right, but who cares? Other people can do what you can't do. You just stick to what God's gifted you to do. He made you just right!"

And the years went by, and I logged up time with God and with my friend, and we have seen Him work miracle after miracle in our lives.

I have the same problem now, but I see a big God. And I see a bigger God all the time. And by golly, I think I'm growing up! In fact, I can't wait to see what I'm going to be when I grow up! God is helping me.

This final description of Moses in Deuteronomy 34:10–12 is wonderful:

> Since then no prophet has risen in Israel like Moses, whom the Lord knew face to face, who did all those miraculous signs and wonders the Lord sent him to do in Egypt—to Pharaoh and to all his officials and to his whole land. For no one has ever shown the mighty power or performed the awesome deeds that Moses did in the sight of all Israel.

Christian, do you want to grow and keep on growing?
You may sometime tell God, "I can't."
But just don't ever tell Him, "I won't."

Questions for Review

1. What is the point of the author's summary of Moses' life?
2. If a feeling of inferiority can cripple us, what can we do about it?
3. What place does obedience have in our growth as Christians?

TWELVE

Lord, Fill Me With Your Power

For background, first read Ephesians 5:1–20

"Don't you know that you yourselves are God's temple and that God's Spirit lives in you?"

1 Corinthians 3:16

Suppose I go down the street with a fifty-dollar bill in my pocket. I don't owe it to anybody, I haven't any desperate needs, it's clear cash. I whistle down the street! I could buy a steak dinner; I could buy a shirt; I could buy a beautiful tie . . . I could buy 'em all, maybe. Fifty bucks! I put my hand in my pocket, and it's a nice feeling.

But, listen, if I've got fifty thousand dollars in my pocket, that does something to me which is vastly different. I walk carefully. I act carefully. There is a new sense of awe and importance about what I'm doing.

Christian, since the moment you came to Christ, you've had the Holy Spirit of God inside of you. And Paul says you can never act the same again. You can never do the things you did before.

Be careful! You are now a temple indwelt by God the Spirit. Let that roll around in your mind a bit. I tell you, that's awesome. Wherever you go, you now carry this "Paraclete," says the Greek—this glorious reservoir of power and praise and love.

Now to him who is able to do immeasurably more than all we ask or imagine,

according to his power that is at work within us,

to him be glory in the church and in Christ Jesus throughout all generations, forever and ever! Amen (Ephesians 3:20,21).

You have been invaded by an outside environment! The Spirit of the Lord has come upon you, and has made your personal little world His sanctuary.

"Be Filled With the Spirit" (Ephesians 5:18)

Notice what happened first when the church was born in Acts chapter two: "All of them were filled with the Holy Spirit" (2:4).

Now see what happened to some of the same people a few days later: "Peter, filled with the Holy Spirit . . ." (Acts 4:8) and "They were all filled with the Holy Spirit . . ." (4:31) and ". . . seven men . . . full of the Spirit . . ." (6:3). They were "born again" only once, but they were filled with the Spirit many times.

What does being "filled" mean? Don't you suppose it must mean being "up to here" with Him—overflowing with awareness of Him and all He's doing in your life at the moment, and receiving Him into your life as totally as you know how at that time?

Ephesians 5:18 has a continuing verb; it really means "be continually being filled with the Spirit."

You ask how the same people can get filled and then filled again?

What if you fill a barrel with watermelons? It's full, isn't it? But then you could fill it again with pecans.

And you could fill it again with sugar.

And you could fill it again with water. . . .

The more you grow in Him, the more you can be filled with Him. Many times before I preach, or I talk to someone, or I do a job, I pray, "Lord, fill me again right now with Your Holy Spirit."

Each time in the Book of Acts when believers were filled, they *said*, they spoke, they witnessed, they opened their mouths. Filling is not just to feel good, to get a "high," but to serve, to witness, to declare, to be God's person.

The New Testament lifestyle was the Spirit-filled life. I believe it's the normal life that God wants every one of us to have.

It's abnormal not to be a Spirit-filled Christian! The disciples were filled, and they were filled again, and they were filled again I'm sure they got empty; I'm sure they fell on their faces;

I'm sure they disappointed others and God and themselves. And they had to come back in repentance many times and be filled again. The filling of the Spirit doesn't mean you're perfect; it simply means that in that moment, as best you know, you're walking in obedience to God.

Ephesians 5:18 actually gives you a choice. It says, "Do not get drunk on wine, which leads to debauchery. Instead, be filled with the Spirit."

I know a man who says he gets drunk because it's the quickest way out of town he knows.

Well, you can choose to "get loaded," but that leads to debauchery, to dissipation. Or you can choose to be filled with the Holy Spirit, which leads to control and to vitality.

You must make that choice. In fact you probably already have today. One writer said, "All Christians belong, in their spiritual experience in growth, somewhere along the scale between immaturity and maturity."

Maturity involves two things: time, and continued control of the Spirit. So a person may be immature for two reasons: either he hasn't been a Christian very long, or else he hasn't been filled with the Spirit and therefore hasn't experienced much growth.

How a Christian Gets Filled With the Spirit

How can you really be all God wants you to be? *There must be desire.*

"If a man is thirsty," said Jesus in John 7:37, "let him come to me and drink." You must want to be filled with God!

Get sick of being an empty believer; get really sick of being self-centered! Get a longing to be Spirit-filled, Christ-centered! The Holy Spirit will always lead you to be centered on Christ. Hate anything else but that!

You're not filled as an inanimate *glass* is filled, as if you don't have anything to do with it—as though you just sit there and God pours in His blessing.

You may be filled as a *house* is filled, with all the life, activities, the sounds, and the joys of the owner going on inside the house. That's a pretty good illustration, but it still isn't enough, because you see, the Holy Spirit is a Person. (Never call Him *it*.)

And you are a person, not a glass or a house. So He comes to blend His Person with yours. Maybe we could say, being filled with Him is being filled with His personality. He comes to give you insight, to give you inspiration, to help you to have love and joy and peace and long-suffering and goodness and gentleness and self-control. The Holy Spirit wants to come into your will and *make you want God*, and want more and more of Him.

> Do you not know, [Paul writes again to the Corinthians] that your body is a temple of the Holy Spirit, who is in you, whom you have received from God? You are not your own; you were bought at a price. Therefore honor God with your body (1 Corinthians 6:19,20).

To know that His Spirit is in you gives you a different mindset. Others may do this or that with their bodies, you can't. Paul follows with a whole chapter (1 Corinthians 7) about being married or single, in the light of this truth about your body. "You are not your own; you can't just live as you please; you have to live under the lordship of that indwelling One."

The Spirit has been released, poured out into your life. Don't grieve Him! (Ephesians 4:30).

And don't limit Him; don't let sin come into your life to dampen and quench that fabulous Potential within you. As 1 Thessalonians 5:19 says, "Don't put out His fire!"

I was reading the Book of Nehemiah this last week. God's temple had been rebuilt and the wall around the city had been restored, and you'd say the Israelites were at last ready to just live flat-out for God.

But compromise crept in. When Nehemiah had a trip out of town, one of the priests allowed treacherous old Tobias to move into one of the rooms in God's holy temple—the very temple that Tobias had tried to keep them from building!

When Nehemiah returned he heard the news, and he literally threw all of Tobias' things out of that temple room, and had the place ceremonially cleansed.

> Christian, throw your sins
> out of God's temple!

Eject any enemies from your life. Toss out all the old trappings. Get them out!

It's scary that a lot of people these days say "I believe" and claim the experience of being born again—and their lives don't seem any different. One day the Lord may say to them, "Depart from me; I never knew you."

Genuine Christianity makes radical changes. In Ephesus, when the name of the Lord Jesus came to be "held in high honor,"

> Many of those who believed now came and openly confessed their evil deeds. A number who had practiced sorcery brought their scrolls together and burned them publicly. When they calculated the value of the scrolls, the total came to fifty thousand drachmas [about fifty thousand days' wages!].
>
> In this way the word of the Lord spread widely and grew in power (Acts 19:18–20).

Christian, your body is God's temple.
Let the temple of God be the temple only *of God.*

List the sins now plaguing you.

_____

_____

_____

_____

_____

_____

_____

_____

"Father, I know that harboring these sins will keep me from the fullness of Your Holy Spirit in my life. And I acknowledge that the fullness of Your Holy Spirit in my life will keep me from harboring these sins.

"Then Holy Spirit, come into my life at this moment, and fill me and cleanse me completely.

"And may this be the beginning of seeking Your refilling and recleansing as often as You prompt me to seek them. In Jesus' Name,

Signed _____

Date _____."

Questions for Review

1. What does it mean to be filled with the Spirit?
2. How many times does a person need to be filled with the Holy Spirit?
3. What can interfere with our being filled?

THIRTEEN

Lord, I Believe;
Help My Unbelief!

For background, first read Hebrews 11

" 'Now I'll give you something to believe,' said the Queen. 'I'm a hundred and one, five months and a day.'

" 'I can't believe that,' said Alice.

" 'Can't you?' the Queen said in a pitying tone. 'Try again; draw a long breath, and shut your eyes.'

"Alice laughed. 'There's no use trying,' she said. 'One can't believe impossible things.'

" 'I dare say you haven't had much practice,' said the Queen. 'When I was your age, I always did it for half an hour a day. Why sometimes I've believed as many as six impossible things before breakfast.' "[10]

There are a lot of strange ideas about living by faith—that it's stepping out of reality and into something heroic, courageous, and a little crazy! That it's believing almost impossible things.

Like the boy in the Sunday school class who was asked to define faith, and he said, "Faith is believing what you know isn't true"!

> Definition of faith: "Now faith is being sure of what we hope for and certain of what we do not see. . . . And without faith it is impossible to please God" (Hebrews 11:1,6).

Jesus modeled it for you:

> Let us fix our eyes on Jesus, the author and perfecter of our faith, who for the joy set before him endured the cross, scorning its shame, and sat down at the right hand of the throne of God.
>
> Consider him who endured such opposition from sinful men, so that you will not grow weary and lose heart (Hebrews 12:2,3).

Christian, expect suffering.
Expect opposition.
Expect misunderstanding.
Your trust in Christ has already made you totally unlike the world, and there is no point in trying to cross back over the bridge.

Here you are, a person with saving faith in the midst of an *un-faith* world. Your challenge is now not to crumble and cave in, but to grow ever more strong and steady in your faith.

... To say, "Lord, do with me whatever You want. I trust You."

... To look your hardships right in the eye and say, "God loves me; He's giving me this for a reason, and He won't test me more than I can take."

... To stand strong and calm in storms with a heart full of cheer and optimism!

". . . Who for the joy set before him endured. . . ."

Remember those earlier days after you had received the light, when you stood your ground in a great contest in the face of suffering. . . .

Do not throw away your confidence; it will be richly rewarded. You need to persevere so that when you have done the will of God, you will receive what he has promised. For in just a very little while, "He who is coming will come and will not delay" (Hebrews 10:32,35–37).

Unfaith operates only within what it can see in the present.

Unfaith is cautious, it's shaky, it's trial and error, it's the best the world can do. God says that that route is unworthy of you, Christian.

Faith Acts

Faith looks straight into God's promises—and steps out and conquers vast territories.

Faith is the bridge connecting your present experiences with the future you hope for. It links your seen with your unseen; it brings eternity into your time. Faith is the way God travels into your present life and ministers to you there.

Sure, in one way faith is a blessed tranquilizer. Confidence in God eases the pain of day-by-day hurts.

But it's more! Many in this world are immobilized by pain
You are freed by faith to move, to live, to go. You can accept
challenges that really cut a wide swath in this world.

By faith Noah built an ark and saved himself and his family
(Hebrews 11:7).

By faith Abraham stepped out and traveled even when he
didn't know where he was going—and received for himself and
his descendants a fabulous land (Hebrews 11:8–10).

By faith Moses' parents were unafraid of their king's death
edict and saved their new baby's life—so that he could become
a great leader (Hebrews 11:23).

"By faith the prostitute Rahab, because she welcomed the
spies, was not killed with those who were disobedient" (Hebrews 11:31).

Caution, fear, unbelief is totally dangerous. Day-by-day faith
in God is totally without risk.

*[The Israelites] were not able to enter, because of their
unbelief* (Hebrews 3:19).

A whole generation of Israelites believed God enough to get
out of the slavery of Egypt behind them, but didn't trust Him
enough to walk into the abundance of the Promised Land ahead
of them.

You have already trusted God enough to turn from the slavery
of your old life without Christ; will you believe in Him enough
to walk through the gates before you of total surrender and total
commitment? Struggle, abundance, and glory lie beyond!

Tell Him about it.

"Lord, I have faith; keep me where my faith fails"
(Mark 9:24 paraphrase).

Signed _____

Date _____

Questions for Review

1. What is the essential ingredient we must have to begin our Christian life?
2. What was the one secret shared by Noah, Abraham, Moses, and Rahab?
3. How do we gain a stronger faith in God?

Where Is God?

Around you (Psalm 125:2)
Above you (Deuteronomy 4:39)
Beneath you (Deuteronomy 33:27)
Before you (Exodus 13:21)
Behind you (Isaiah 52:12)
With you (Isaiah 41:10)
For you (Romans 8:31)
On your right hand (Isaiah 41:13)
Near you (Psalm 145:18)
In you (Colossians 1:27)
Living with you (Isaiah 57:15)
His eye is upon you (Psalm 33:18)

He is "all—and in all"

Hallelujah!

P.S.

Sometimes on Monday mornings a typical little boy doesn't feel well, and he can't get out of bed and go to school.

What he needs is the miracle of the *healing of desire.*

If you say to him, "Forget school, let's go swimming" he will spring out of bed; he's suddenly well.

In the old days of your own life you could have looked at sections of this book—

praying,
    loving,
        giving,

worshiping,
        studying, and so on—
and you'd say, "I don't feel well."

Now you have the Holy Spirit within!
He has performed the miracle of
the healing of desire,
and you can spring
out of your lethargy.

But the "swimming hole" you love and will go back and back to is even better than you think. It's being filled and filled and filled . . . with a source, a great spring a roaring waterfall of newness.

You can enjoy from now to always God's vast powers for your continuing renewal.

God bless you, Christian, on this Monday morning of your life.

Would you let me know how you're doing? Write to:

Ray Ortlund
Renewal Ministries
32 Whitewater Drive
Corona del Mar, CA 92625

NOTES

1 Chapter 1, page 14: Andrew Murray, *The Two Covenants* (Old Tappan, NJ: Fleming H. Revell Company), 1974, pages 165,166.

2. Chapter 1, page 15: *See* my books *Lord, Make My Life a Miracle* (Regal Books, 2300 Knoll Drive, Ventura, CA 93003, 1974) and *Three Priorities for a Strong Local Church* (Word Books, Irving, TX 75039, 1983, 1988).

3. Chapter 1, page 18: Anne Ortlund, *Discipling One Another* (Irving, TX: Word Books), 1979.

4. Chapter 2, page 29: Anne Ortlund, *Up With Worship* (Ventura, CA: Regal Books), 1975.

5. Chapter 5, page 65: Anne Ortlund, *Disciplines of the Beautiful Woman* (Irving, TX: Word Books), 1977. *See* especially pages 71-73.

6. Chapter 7, pages 91,92: Arnold Lobel, *Frog and Toad Together* (New York: Harper & Row, Publishers, Inc.), 1972.

7. Chapter 8, page 104: *See* my book *Lord, Make My Life a Miracle.*

8. Chapter 8, page 109: Anne Ortlund, *Children Are Wet Cement* (Old Tappan, NJ: Fleming H. Revell Company), 1981.

9. Chapter 8, page 110: *See* Anne's book *Discipling One Another.*

10. Chapter 13, page 175: Lewis Carroll, *Through the Looking Glass* (New York: Grosset and Dunlap, Inc.), 1946.

About the Author

Respected evangelical pastor and teacher Raymond C. Ortlund graduated from the University of Puget Sound in 1947 and Princeton Theological Seminary in 1950. Ordained a Presbyterian minister, he has pastored churches in Pennsylvania, New York, and California. He has ministered in North and South America, Europe, Australia, Asia, and Africa to all sorts of believers, including native Hawaiians, persecuted Christians in Afghanistan, and Eskimos living in the northernmost inhabited spot in the world.

He is the author of *Lord, Make My Life a Miracle, Intersections, Three Priorities for a Strong Local Church,* and with his wife, Anne, *The Best Half of Life, You Don't Have to Quit, Renewal,* and *Confident in Christ.*

Dr. Ortlund is also the president and main speaker of the "Haven of Rest" international radio broadcast. The Ortlunds have four children, all in Christian ministry, and they live in Newport Beach, California.